War in Heaven and Earth

Hugh B. Black

New Wine Press

New Wine Press
PO Box 17
Chichester
West Sussex
PO20 6YB
England

Unless otherwise stated, all biblical references are taken from the Revised Version of the Bible.

ISBN: 1 874367 55 8

Other books by Hugh Black:

The Baptism in the Spirit and Its Effects
Reflections on the Gifts of the Spirit
Reflections on a Song of Love (1 Corinthians 13)
A Trumpet Call to Women
The Clash of Tongues: With Glimpses of Revival
Consider Him (Twelve Qualities of Christ)
Battle for the Body
The Incomparable Christ
Gospel Vignettes
Reflections from Abraham
Reflections from Moses: With the Testimony of Dan McVicar
Christ the Deliverer
Christian Fundamentals
Reflections from David
Pioneers of the Spiritual Way
Revival: Including the Prophetic Vision of Jean Darnall
Revival: Personal Encounters
Revival: Living in the Realities
E.H. Taylor: A Modern Christian Mystic (edited by Hugh Black)

Typeset by CRB Associates, Lenwade, Norwich.
Printed in England by Clays Ltd, St Ives plc.

Dedication

To those of my colleagues
who know not only the theory but the reality
of deep spiritual warfare – who stand
constant in prayer against the forces of darkness and
who uphold leaders as Aaron and Hur upheld Moses.

Acknowledgements

My thanks go those of my friends and family who have helped in the production of various drafts of this book: my wife Isobel, my daughter Alison, Pauline Anderson and Jennifer Jack.

Appreciation is also due to the large number of people who have allowed me to use their testimonies and other spoken or written contributions.

I am particularly indebted to Sovereign World Ltd for permission to quote extensively from C. Peter Wagner, ed., *Territorial Spirits* in chapter 5 of my own study.

Contents

Foreword

In our spiritual walk, there comes across our path from time to time a book which can totally change our outlook on a subject, or shed light on an area of which we have only had the vaguest, if any, knowledge at all. *War in Heaven and Earth* may well prove to be just such a book to many who read the truths which lie within its pages.

As some of the chapter headings reveal, the battle is not only in the heavenly but also in the earthly realm. The author's treatment will alert many to the 'natural' devices that Satan uses to attempt to bring about our spiritual downfall.

The chapters on territorial spirits are fascinating. Mr Black draws on experiences from within his own circle, as well as others recorded by men of God from various parts of the world. 'Real life places' have been named and hard evidence is documented of 'before and after' situations as the battle for the places on earth has been fought and won in the spiritual realm. Especially interesting to me was the mention of Germany, as back in 1990 while travelling through Munich I became acutely aware of a terrible evil and darkness in that city; a very cold grip. As I stood in the main railway station scanning the faces of the throng, there was knowledge of an awful hardness in those who passed by. I pray God that one day that very city will be mentioned among the 'before and after' and that Christ who is Lord over all shall reign supreme.

In travelling between Northern Ireland and Eire in 1995 (both of which have strong but very different controlling spirits), there came the revelation that although the natural (political) border between the North and South followed a particular path, the spiritual border followed quite a different route and the spiritual territory of the North extended several miles over the border in the South.

These incidents of which I have had personal experience and the many more mentioned in the book will be an entirely new concept to many a Christian. But I trust that God will use them to bring a fresh realization to the reader that our battle is not with flesh and blood: but as we stand in the glorious victory of the Lord Jesus Christ, we shall see these dark powers brought low and our Jesus lifted high above all.

Susie Jean Sharkey

Introduction

In November 1993 I was asked to take a series of four seminars on the theme of Spiritual Warfare.[1]

The invitation came at a time when I had already published a certain amount on the subject in two earlier books. Other material, as yet unpublished, lay ready to be transcribed from conference tapes. And there was a new area which as yet I had scarcely explored at all but whose significance immediately began to grip me.

The material fell naturally into four sections. The first was spiritual warfare down at earth level, which had been dealt with in *Revival: Living in the Realities*. The second section was related to the weapons of our warfare (and these are not restricted to the list in Ephesians where we are enjoined to put on the whole armour of God); this had been our camp/conference theme in July 1993. The third section concerned the whole subject of deliverance (much of which was covered in *Christ the Deliverer*) and included the controversial topic of demonic activity in the lives of Christians. The fourth section was one on which I had general ideas and some experience but a lack of detailed information: this meant that I had to do a bit of hard work and research the subject.

The subject in question was that of principalities and powers, with territorial spirits and their influence. And as I began to read, God began to speak to me and I realized that I was not merely reading for the sake of lecturing at four seminars. As I was reading, I was learning, and God was speaking in my spirit. I began to see that so often our strategy in opposing Satan is wrong.

Let me give you a foreglimpse into the subject by a brief comment at this point on the mistaken strategy. It is of particular significance. We have forgotten the command of Christ that *before we destroy the strong man's goods we must first bind the strong man.* And evidence has accumulated across the world that before attempting the evangelization of heathen lands this has frequently not been done. Often men and women have laboured for many years without seeing a soul saved. In some cases there has come the revelation that they were going the wrong way about their work. Instead of grappling with the central dominant power of evil over an area, they had been trying again and again to gather fruit, and when the new concept came and intercessors had power over malignant spirits dominant in particular areas and broke their power, salvation came in floods: by the thousand souls were born.

I suddenly thought, 'I have lived here in the Greenock area all my life, and there is a dominant spirit of darkness that has bound much of the gospel through all the years.' And I looked forward to the day when intercessors should be able to break the power of that dominant evil and the windows of heaven should open upon us. To the seminar participants I suggested that they consider the series not so much a means of intellectual instruction, but rather a means in the hand of God of opening up our area to the power of the living God.

And that is the same spirit in which I would have you read this book, which comprises the four themes indicated above.[2] To that end I have included a considerable amount of up-to-date testimony to God's healing and delivering power. Some of these stories are narrated by those in our midst who are experienced in various aspects of the ministry of deliverance and the warring with dark powers that accompanies it. Chapter 6 in particular includes quite phenomenal elements. A commentary on one of its episodes is provided in chapter 7, which consists of a sermon preached by my daughter, Mrs Grace Gault, shortly after the event described. This message came with exceptional clarity and power and is a fitting conclusion to the theme of spiritual warfare.

As in my more recent books there is an attempt to take readers into the services or seminars where much of the material was first presented. This explains the inclusion of prayers, prophecies and linking comments.

Notes

[1] The Rev. William Wilson, then minister of George Square Baptist Church, Greenock, was responsible for the idea and organization of the Seminars on Spiritual Warfare. A man of unusual humility, Bill had occasionally come into our Saturday night services and had shared in the blessing of God that was in the atmosphere – an atmosphere where a person could be healed in a moment of time, with or without any laying on of hands or personal ministry, an atmosphere where people went through into the glory of God. Bill had wanted that to spread across the town, and that, I think, is why he had used his influence to arrange the seminar series.

[2] To give the present writing cohesion some of the earlier material is again used, as are some illustrations of particular principles that have appeared in one or other of my earlier books. I was faced with a problem – whether to leave out all previously published material and include instead a list of references to where particular items might be found, or to put it all in with the acute realization that some of the material would appear familiar to certain readers. Not to include the material here would disadvantage new readers, and so on balance we have left it in.

Chapter 1

Battle at Ground Level

Prayer: Lord, we realize that in coming to this particular subject we come against the principalities and the powers and the rulers of darkness. But, O God, we fear them not because we trust Christ. Neither do we treat them lightly, and we would be lost in Christ; we would be under the deep anointing of the Holy Spirit. O Lord our God, we pray for the moving of Your power, for the deep drawing near of the Lord, that there may be an opening into these vital subjects, that we may learn, and not only learn at the mind level, but understand at a spiritual level, that we may be the better equipped to go forward in the things of the kingdom. We ask it, O God, in the name Lord Jesus Christ, and for His sake. Amen.

In our first study we deal with issues that many may not recognize as having anything to do with spiritual warfare.

Mundane Matters

We start not at the top, not with the high-level powers operating in a dimension beyond the experience of most of us, but we start down low, right around our feet at the earth level: considering the kinds of situations that you and I are meeting from day to day and often not recognizing as spiritual warfare at all.

Let me tell you how preaching about spiritual warfare started for me. God had been with us over a period, and I had been taking a series on revival, much of which is now published. Immediately after concluding the series I preached a sermon on spiritual warfare, and had you asked me to put my sermons in order of my own estimate of their impact or importance, I think I might have put that one near the bottom of the list. But then I noticed that more people came to me after that sermon and talked about it and expressed appreciation than perhaps for any sermon for years. Now our congregation is not composed of people who come and express appreciation readily. But I noticed the number of them who did come, and it caused me to reflect. And I followed the first sermon with a second on the same subject. It seemed to me to be an exceptionally simple presentation, but of course quite often deep spiritual things are not in fact unduly complex.

Evangelical and Pentecostal Viewpoints

I know that I am addressing an evangelical company. I imagine that most of us are believers. We may be of different shades of doctrine, but we are believers, and probably have the same kind of basic attitude to spiritual warfare. For most of us this is probably fairly vague: there is God on the throne and there is his arch-enemy Satan, who was created by God. He rebelled against God and took with him perchance a third of the angels (cf. Revelation 12:4). They have continued their rebellion, and there is war between God and the devil, between good and evil, and it is pursued on earth. We believe that God will be triumphant and Satan will be bound and ultimately consigned to the lake of fire. It is evident from the New Testament that in Christ's day Satan's emissaries, the demons, were very active. They were seen as inhabiting the bodies of men and women, and the Gospels speak of Christ casting them out.

14

After an area of general agreement we come on to points about which there is greater difference. There are some who believe that the casting out of demons and pentecostal phenomena generally were for the beginning of the dispensation only, while others strongly hold that with Christ going back to the glory there was no indication that demons were immediately expelled worldwide from all men, or that the need for exorcism ceased. Demon possession is seen as a reality that has gone on down the years. Those of us who are in the pentecostal or charismatic traditions are generally very open to the reality of demons actually inhabiting the bodies of men and women and requiring to be cast out.

In recent times, partly through the writings of men like C.S. Lewis (in *The Screwtape Letters*, for example), there has come a deepening consciousness of the action of the wicked one through his emissaries. In *This Present Darkness*, *Piercing the Darkness*, and *The Prophet*, Frank E. Peretti has used the form of the novel to speak of an ongoing contest. Very recently there has been a real wave of interest in spiritual warfare, and one of a number of books which has particularly highlighted the subject is C. Peter Wagner's *Territorial Spirits*, to which later reference will be made. There is also a growing consciousness amongst men and women who are used in this field, that there is deep, ongoing, persistent warfare, and it reaches to a very high level.

Through most of a lifetime many of us have not been particularly conscious of severe satanic onslaught or of warfare at high or heavenly levels, but we have been aware of the devil's activity in our own lives. And I now want to open your eyes to truths in this realm that are not always understood or recognized. There are two things in particular that the devil tries to do. He tries to give wrong pictures, and he lies. He is adept at false representations, and he is the father of lies.

At a later point we will take up the theme of the deeper warfare.

An Interesting Diversion

We shall start right down at a very low level. Consider a man who is delivered from addiction to drugs or alcohol. The war between Satan and his soul commences. And here we meet a problem, one I have never been able to solve. I do not understand why, when the devil has a man on his back, really on his back, it is important to him to sink the man further in the mire. Increasingly and infinitely he will try to push people to deepening levels of evil. What does he get out of it? I don't know. But I thank God there is another picture – and I have never understood this either – the intensity of the care of Christ for one individual. When Christ lays His hand upon a soul He will take him to a higher level, and He will not be satisfied; He will take him to a still higher level, and while life lasts He will be taking him ever upward until he reflects Christ Himself, until Christ is alive in him. Every little detail of our life where holiness is concerned is important to Christ, and every little detail of our increasing wickedness is important to Satan. And it is very difficult to comprehend.

Let me go a little further. Why should it matter to Jesus how one solitary man should react to Him – one man, a speck of dust, not just a speck in the balance, but a speck like one grain of sand against all the sea shores of all the world, one individual – and there are multiplying numbers of humans alive in every generation. Why should one be so important to Christ? Remember that Christ was the creator of the ends of the earth, and Christ was the creator of Peter. And yet you can feel the heartcry of Jesus for that treacherous one: 'Simon, son of John, lovest thou Me?' Peter's love was important to Jesus. I do not understand why it was so important to Him. He had, or was to have, millions of others. It is like the story of the lost sheep. From one point of view Christ was not interested in millions of others who were safe; He was interested in one lost sheep. The degree of His care is difficult to understand. He cares intensely for the individual.

Now on the other side the wicked one cares intensely to keep bound his every serf. You can see the man coming up out of alcoholism, out of drug addiction: he has found Christ. Satan or his emissary comes, and what does he do? He lies to him and gives him a false picture. As the man is sitting pondering, Satan flashes a picture into his mind of a pub, and of the company around the bar, and he reminds him of the taste of alcohol, or the effect of the drug, whatever it may be. He presents that picture to his mind, and into his thought he lies: 'You'll feel better. You'll feel relieved. This pressure will go off you if you just go and take a drink, or if you go and have an injection. You know you're going to do it anyway.' And he lies to him and deceives him with a wrong picture. Again and again the dupe accepts the picture and goes down.

Down to Earth

Now that is spiritual warfare. We recognize that quite clearly. It is not difficult to understand. The difficulty comes at the next level. It is where most of us live, actually. If I were going round a normal Christian company I would find people who would say that they suffer from lack of confidence, and that because of lack of confidence they can't do this, that and the other. They take this as part of their natural heritage. And there are others who would say, 'Well, you know, I was born with a jealous disposition. It is something on which I am vulnerable.' Another would say, 'If someone does me wrong, hatred is stirred in me terribly easily. And I was born that way; I have always been that way.' You can extend the list at your own convenience. But most of you, I am sure, will be able to recognize your own areas of vulnerability, the things on which you are frequently tempted, the things on which you fall. Normally you do not associate this with Satan or his works, but with your own natural dispositions, your flesh and your natural weaknesses. But when you see beyond the surface of things to the way in which the wicked one comes at us through our flesh you begin to look at these matters very differently.

Death to Self

There is a basic Christian doctrine which is not sufficiently taught. It is the doctrine of death to self. The New Testament teaches it. We should reckon ourselves dead, nevertheless alive with Christ in us. Paul teaches this very clearly and plainly. I normally consider the doctrine under three headings: the first, death to the heart and the affections of the heart that do not spring from Christ; the second, death to the will, which is apt to resurrect itself and defy God; and the third, which I consider the most difficult of all three, death to the mind: reckoning your mind dead, submitted to God, coming under the domain, the power of God, letting your mind be garrisoned. In so far as you leave these three areas uncrucified you leave yourself vulnerable to the onslaught of Satan.

Death to the heart

Take, for example, Hudson Taylor, engaged to a lovely girl whom he deeply loved and wanted to marry. She was unwilling to go to China, and he knew the call of God on his life. He sacrificed that love relationship for a higher good, and responded to God's call. Today there are millions of souls in the glory either directly or indirectly as a result of the work of Hudson Taylor. He made sacrifice. He allowed his heart to be crucified. Now any man or woman who does not allow that to happen retains an area of vulnerability. You will find at critical times when God is about to use you that something can go wrong with a love relationship, and you are out of the game; the devil has you on your back.

Death to the will

Perhaps the most remarkable example of this which I have ever witnessed concerned a devoted young lady who had gone on exceptionally well with God. An hour came when she realized that something fundamental was still required. She sought help and I found myself suddenly in a violent and unexpected battle with Satan. In the course of our speaking together before prayer, she made a remark which deeply disturbed me in a way which she would be quite unaware of. So deep was the assault that I had to delay praying. Evidently at that time she knew fear to a level she had never known before and was accusing me in her heart of sitting idly by. At last I got the spiritual grip and got through to God.

Her description of what happened is memorable. God gave her a revelation of her will as He saw it. What had seemed to her previously as no doubt an admirable quality was in fact a thing of horror. She loathed what she saw but then made the horrible discovery that she did not want to yield it to God – in fact felt she could not yield it. I knew she was in the throes of deadly conflict. It was a crisis hour in her life. God, I believe, led me gently and I said, 'While you may not be willing to yield, are you willing to let God make you willing?' She was able to do this, and immediately she was through.

The change this produced in her life was profound. For several days she felt like a person moving around as one dead. She was advised not to try to come out of this condition too quickly, but let the process take its full course. When she did emerge the old dominant will was really broken and her attitudes and reactions to others were radically altered.

It can be done. God changes people.

Death to the mind

I have found the mind the most difficult of all the areas to deal with. I remember so clearly in my own earlier days that again and again just prior to preaching or ministry of some kind, something would come into my mind at the critical point: 'Oh, you have forgotten to deal with that – and, you know, if you don't get through on it, you're not likely to come under anointing and you will not be in good form. You'll need to give attention to it.' I would be diverted and would give attention to the matter, the anointing would fade and I would get into the grip of Satan. I would be bound, and my preaching would be affected. This went on until I learned to take the attitude, 'Is the thought coming from God or myself or the devil?' And if I was not convinced it was coming from God I would say, 'Out! I will not even think about it.' Instead I allowed the anointing of God to come. I learned at least in a measure how to garrison my mind. Now don't misunderstand me. I am not claiming that all is under control. The devil is subtle and strong, and he will return to areas that have been fought over before and attempt to recover lost ground. The mind is very difficult to control, and he will persist along these lines. I deal further with this under 'Introspection' (chapter 2).

Preliminary Skirmishing

Now I want to get right down to very practical levels. Normally there is a dark assault before a time of usefulness. That is an ongoing thing, and I can illustrate it from present circumstances. I was getting along quite well with preparation for this conference; I was looking forward to it – the subject interested me and I knew I would be meeting people who are my friends. I expected to enjoy happy fellowship. I had conducted a funeral service in the afternoon, and God had been with me. It was a very sad case. The man concerned had been unsaved, but two of his sisters were believers. You have to be very tactful and careful at such a funeral. You don't want to speak what is untrue or leave wrong impressions. We cannot put an unbeliever in heaven. But neither does one want to be harsh and unmindful of the feelings of the mourners. Suddenly I found a wonderful way into the subject. After the preliminaries I said, 'You know, this was a very fortunate man.' As the company looked at me, I imagine they would be thinking, 'In what way was he fortunate?' I indicated that he was fortunate in that he had two sisters who had found Christ as Saviour. There are many people who don't have anybody who has found Christ as Saviour, and he had opportunity to find the same way that they found. I had no knowledge that he had found that way, but I knew he had opportunity: he was a fortunate man. It enabled me to open up the whole subject of the gospel, both heaven and hell, without being too pointed. You find that God comes with you in these circumstances. And God was with me. The funeral and the tea which followed would be over between three and four o'clock.

And then the dark one drew near. You will realize I am bringing things right down to earth. I am dealing with the present: not last week, not yesterday, but now.

You say, 'What do you mean by that kind of language, "The dark one drew near"?'

A Demon Sighted

There are various ways in which he draws near. Twice in my life I have seen a demon. Now on the second of these occasions, some years back, I wakened and was conscious of a horrible feeling around my head, a 'yucky' feeling, in modern slang – indeed worse than yucky; it was a black yuckiness, if you can understand what that means. I wakened in time to see the demon – not just with interior vision but with my eyes open. The demon was horrible, absolutely horrible. As I glimpsed it, it was actually receding at high speed right out through the opposite wall of my room. But I had time to see it and feel it, and could feel its atmosphere and influence. As a result I walked very carefully, waiting for ensuing consequences. That is one way in which the dark one can draw near.

More Subtle Approaches

But that is not the way in which he normally draws near

to me. He does not normally herald his presence. He doesn't have hoofs and horns. He comes rather in a very reasonable way, as he came to Eve and said (if I may paraphrase), 'Now wait a wee minute, Eve. *Hath God said* – do you think God really meant you not to eat of that tree? Don't you realize that when you do it you'll be better off – you'll be more like God? God would really want you, you know, to be more like Him, to know not only good but good and evil – you will be like a god.'

'Right enough, there is something in that,' she might have thought.

A subtle approach. And again and again he draws near as an angel of light and he places before you something that is attractive, that could be a good thing, and yet deep down in you there is a feeling of a green snake somewhere, and a lurid light somewhere, and something not just right somewhere. You see, he doesn't come and ask a good Christian to go to a black magic circle or to attend a sabbat or to get involved in witchcraft: that would have no appeal whatever.

A Wrong Push Upwards

I remember the late Duncan Campbell telling me of a very illuminating incident. He was in the very heart of revival; people were being saved, revival was ongoing, the Bible was a talking book. And he said, 'You know, the devil used a new device.' Paul could say, *We are not ignorant of his devices* (2 Corinthians 2:11). I would like to be able to say that, but he catches me too often on new devices. Duncan Campbell said a strange thing happened. 'Normally', he said, 'the devil tried to pull me down, but this time he pushed me up, and I entered a spiritual plane, a dimension with which I was not familiar. It was presented as a good place and one to be desired. Suddenly I found that the Bible stopped speaking to me, and revival began to dry up around me.' Evidently he was not conscious at that point of sin. But because of what was happening he gave attention to his personal life, and he found an area in which I think he felt he had transgressed. He did not reveal the detail, but he said, 'I had to accept a severe discipline in my life, and it was exceedingly severe, until I got back to the place I had been in previously, where the Bible had been a talking book and revival fire burned.'

You will not always recognize Satan in his approach. He will approach at an earthly plane on earthly things dealing with your human emotions, your feelings, your desires. And he will approach as an angel of light. He will suggest 'a better way'.

Battle Commences

So you are saying by now, 'And what did he do to you today?' Well, I believe Rabbie Burns can be criticized for an awful lot of what he did. But there are a few lines he wrote of which I do approve. I commend them thoroughly:

> Aye free, aff han' your story tell,
> When wi' a bosom crony,
> But still keep somethin' to yoursel'
> Ye scarcely tell to ony.

So I will follow that piece of advice and only tell you the bit that I feel like telling you!

He drew near. Now I didn't recognize him.

You say, 'You've been on the road a long time: why didn't you recognize him?' Well, I'll leave you to answer that question yourselves when you get to my age.

There came a suggestion into my mind about something that had deeply pained me some little time ago. It was something that touched me very deeply. Many of you would probably have thought it quite irrational, but to me it wasn't irrational; it was very reasonable, and it caused me very real pain. God had previously intervened, and I had been able to cast my burden on the Lord, and He healed my spirit. Suddenly the matter came back into my mind, and it came back with a supernatural force behind it: a demand to give attention to it. I knew that at a human level I would never come to terms with the matter. My whole life could be affected by it. I was greatly tempted to take the devil's part and reconsider the whole incident – to reopen a wound that God had healed. But I stopped. I realized the strategy of Satan: I realized that a meeting was coming up, I saw the subtlety of the attack, and I did what I had had to do months earlier: I cast myself on God to hear what He had to say, to get the revelation that came directly from Him. And the thing was a lie; the situation was not as it was being presented. The devil's picture was a total lie, the devil's suggestion was a total lie, and God said, 'You can let your spirit go free. There is no such thing as you fear.'

Now that is spiritual warfare. Some people get the idea that spiritual warfare is merely a matter of quietly praying that God will save this one and that one and the other, and of speaking to Him about various needs and afflictions. Friends, there's a lot more to spiritual warfare than that. I'm not saying that shouldn't go on. But spiritual warfare can be in rather a different dimension.

Into the Attack

I realize that so much of what I have said to you at the moment is negative. It deals with that side of the war that is carried into your camp by the devil. But, you know, we are supposed to carry the war into his camp. I will be dealing with that later in considering the 'Weapons of our Warfare', and will only touch on the subject here. In many congregations in various parts of the country God has His chosen intercessors – people who have gone beyond being merely interested in their own spiritual condition, and have become involved in carrying the war into Satan's territory. These people live in such a way that they carry burdens that come from God. They come into situations where the Holy Spirit is very near them, and He whispers to them, and He lays burden upon them. I know of various people (and I can speak with experience here) who come under intense burden for a situation, for an individual, or for some aspect of God's work. When that burden comes there is nothing they can do about it, in the sense of dismissing it happily, or hurrying its outworking. Indeed they have the sense of not doing anything, but of something happening through them. They do battle with Satan and are faithful, and God is victorious through them. It is difficult for many people to understand how this functions.

I remember being involved in my early days in open-air work. God really blessed us. People were talking about burdens of prayer, and I remember thinking, 'Well, I'm leading this open-air, and I don't have any burden of prayer.' I remember mentioning my lack of burden to one whom many of you will remember, Miss Taylor,[1] and she looked at me and said, 'You might not have any burden of prayer, but there are other people who do.' She was a kindly person and did not go on to say, 'And don't ever get it into your head that everything is swinging round about you.' We have to remember that God has many servants in the field; there are often many people involved in a work of God. While one might have a preaching commission, another might have a very deep burden of prayer.

I don't think I ever personally realized what a burden of prayer was until I went to the island of Lewis. God moved in great power on that island. I first went there as the result of a letter that came from a friend. On reading it I had the knowledge that God could do something about a particular situation if I was there. I went, and within twenty-four hours of my being on the island, He spoke to me as clearly as I am speaking to you.[2] He spoke as with an audible voice in my spirit. He empowered and commissioned me. I went to my lodgings and came under a burden of prayer for the first time in my life. And you know, I didn't want to move from an old armchair; I knelt before it, hour after hour. I didn't want to eat, I didn't want to sleep, I didn't want to talk. I had nothing I wanted to do but let this burden rest upon me and work its way through me. This may have gone on for a day or two, and then suddenly I knew I was through to God. I got up and went to the home of the person for whose sake I had gone to Lewis. God was with me. The message was received and the door was open, and through that open door many other doors opened all over the island. God moved, and people were filled with the Holy Spirit. I realized the connection between prayer burden and the outworking of the purposes of God. It was wonderful. The prayer element was vital. God carried the war into the territory of the enemy.

Your Areas of Weakness

But for this session I want you to ponder a little so that you may receive all that I can transmit. Where is your area of vulnerability? Where does the devil get at you? Through what are you particularly discouraged? Where are the points of weakness which you need strengthened? From the moment in which you realize his action in exploiting your weakness, and the readiness of Christ to strengthen you on the weak points, you are in a position to do battle. And it is not a matter of your going forward to engage the enemy. It is a matter of going into Christ and seeing Him fight Satan through you. Let me say a controversial thing at this point. Most people think that it is their duty to fight Satan, and to pursue him, and to pray about their problems. I don't believe that. I have shocked many a group by this statement. Never pray about a problem.

You say, 'Wait a minute, that's unreasonable; you're going over the top.' No, I'm not going over the top. Do look at your problem: take a good look at it, and then look to Christ – and never again look at your problem. Have you ever noticed, if you have a problem and you focus on it, it deepens? And as you pray about it you keep it at the forefront of your mind, and before you know where you are the devil can entangle you and drag you down on your problem. What do you do? Recognize it before Christ: say, 'There it is, Lord.' Your solution is not by pursuing it. Your solution is found in going into God, into Christ. And as you do this, the problem begins to diminish, and His power comes against it. Too often we are like a drowning man obsessed by his plight and threshing around to his own destruction. When his rescuer comes he should totally relax and trust him to save him. There comes a point where he himself can do nothing. So it is in the things of God. You stand with Christ and you see the problem shrivel before the power of Christ. Spiritual problems are not solved by us. We may at intellectual levels try, and frequently find ourselves in confusion. Problems are solved by the power of Christ focusing on them, and that is an entirely different matter.

You Have a Destiny

I sometimes preach under the heading, 'You have a Destiny'. Every individual born has a destiny. There is a place for you to achieve under God that is for no one else – for no one else ever born or ever to be born. There is something God wants in and for you that is unique. There is a reflection of Christ that He wants to shine from your life that will be different from His reflection from any other life. There is a savour of Christ to come from you as an individual that will never come from anybody else in all the world. Recently I was presented with a real problem. I became aware of a mature Christian suddenly realizing something in this realm that I never for a moment thought would not have been understood and known. And this may be of value to others. Mark what I say. This mature and deeply used Christian had never fully realized that she had a destiny, a birthright with which no one could interfere, that no matter how many gifted people arose it had nothing whatever to do with the call of God on her life; there was a completion in Christ for her that could never be more complete.

Each one is loved as an individual. God cares for us all and He will protect our every interest. He will take every point of weakness and will come in and strengthen and flow through us. Friend, you can attain the stars. I believe that every man and woman has a destiny if we will only accept it, a birthright if we will only enter into it. There are no favourites with God, and to underline that truth the New Testament says very clearly,

> *Elijah was a man of like passions with us, and he prayed
> . . . and it rained not . . . And he prayed again . . . and the
> heaven gave rain . . .*   (James 5:17–18)

In other words, the God of Elijah is our God, and what Elijah accomplished through God can encourage us in our turn to expect God's purposes to be fully outworked through us. You can attain the heights that Elijah knew. I actually believe that every man and woman born, if they will commit themselves wholly to God in every sense of that word, can reach the high, wonderful heights of God. The door is open to every son and daughter of Adam's race. I am a total optimist; I believe what I say. I really believe it, and I thank God that I do.

I have known people come in amongst us who have seemed very unpromising. You might have said, 'That person will never go far.' But I tell you, when the power of God came upon them, they were transformed. God really changes men and women. And the day I stop believing that, I stop preaching. I don't care where you are now. God can change you, blessed be His name. He can come into every area of weakness that the devil exploits, and you can find total victory in the spiritual warfare that goes on around you from day to day.

It is in familiar, everyday situations that much of your warfare is conducted. People annoy you, people get at you, you can't stand them: Satan comes in on these avenues and you don't recognize it, but that's how he comes in.

His Body to be Intact

I remember a missionary home on furlough from India telling me of how she and her colleagues were intensely annoyed at a fellow missionary. Oh, how annoying their sister was! It got to the stage that the very way she took her soup was too much for the others. Her teeth clacked, and they couldn't stand it. Her behaviour was atrocious, and they wanted her cut off. They were about to take steps to have her removed when one of them in a vision saw Christ, and the tip of His little finger was just hanging by a thread. God made it very clear that the despised sister was part of His body and He wanted a whole body. There was to be healing and not severance.

Righteous Indignation

Have you ever had righteous indignation? Oh, I know what righteous indignation is. Don't I just! I remember one of my co-workers seemed to me to be behaving abominably on a particular occasion; I don't remember now what it was about, but it seemed like that to me. And we had a right how-d'ye-do before I was due to preach one Sunday morning. I thought, 'It's all right for you; I've got the preaching to do!' And I was really annoyed. She got up and led the singing as though she hadn't a care in the world, while I was sitting at her back fuming. And do you know, God convicted me of my reaction. He never said a word to me as to whether she was right or wrong – I still think she was wrong, but God never said a word about that.

But He took the bitterness out of my heart, and the anger.

On another occasion years later, a fellow worker acted in a way that I felt was very unfair. God spoke to me very clearly. He didn't say whether the person was right or wrong (He never did tell me anything like that; He always told me, however, when I was wrong). He said, 'You have let love go out of your heart.' Now He didn't mean sentimental love; it was the love of God in the work of God. 'You have stopped having a right attitude.' I said, 'Lord, I'm sorry.' And the moment I repented, He forgave, and restored my soul and my peace. My grievance faded like snow in the sun. Blessed be His name.

Let us always realize that in the very ordinary and mundane matters of life, spiritual warfare takes place. The battle is not always in the heavenlies but right down around our feet.

Notes

[1] Elizabeth H. Taylor was a founder and co-leader of the Struthers fellowship from its inception. For her life and selected sayings see my following publications (all New Dawn Books): Part 2 of *A Trumpet Call to Women* (1988); *E.H. Taylor: A Modern Christian Mystic* (1994); and the Appendix to *Gospel Vignettes* (1989).

[2] For details of this event see my *Revival: Personal Encounters* (New Dawn Books, 1993), chapter 2.

Chapter 2

The Devil's Weapons

Prayer: Lord our God, we can never take anything for granted in a wrong way in the work of God. No matter how often the empowering of the Holy Spirit comes, there never comes a time when we can do these things of ourselves. We are ever dependent on God, and increasingly dependent on God, and we realize it will never be any other way. For we do not want a manifestation of the flesh at any time: only the overflow of the divine, the coming of the word of God that is alive and powerful, sharper than a two-edged sword. Lord our God, we pray that Your power shall continue with us, that You will open up the deep truths of Scripture, and spiritual principle and spiritual law. We ask it, O God, in the Name Lord Jesus Christ and for His sake. Amen.

The Coming of Revelation

When it was suggested to me late last night[1] that I might consider preaching on the strategy of Satan, I had at that time no 'yen' to think around any such subject. Having done a fair share of the ministry in the first part of the week, I thought that I might be more on holiday for the remaining two days of camp, with others carrying the main burden.

But suddenly I felt that God spoke to me, and all thought of holiday was gone. He often does that at critical times: He just gives you a word, it drops into your consciousness and you recognize it; you don't argue about it. And this was a subject on which I had never preached before.

Suddenly, out of the blue, into my mind there fell that phrase: *the weapons of your warfare* (cf. 2 Corinthians 10:3). I hadn't been thinking about weapons or warfare. I was perfectly peaceful. But it came so clearly: *the weapons of your warfare*. And I found I began to get revelation. With such a title you might expect your mind to go to the thought of putting on the whole armour of God mentioned in Ephesians 6. There one of the weapons is offensive, which is the sword, and the rest of that armour is defensive. But that was not in fact the way God opened the subject up to me at all.

Revelation did not come all at once, but in gradual stages. There came the idea of a fight with the devil. There is going to be a duel – a battle, an encounter – with the devil. You know what it was like in an earlier age in this country, and more so on the Continent (in Germany particularly), where duelling was concerned. You said something that offended somebody and they challenged you to a duel. It was the person challenged who had the right to choose the weapons.

I have only once been anywhere near a duel. The occasion was an international conference in Oxford, a very high-powered affair. There were prominent educationalists from the Continent and from this country. I was there as a representative of a national committee. The various nationals did not get on too well together, and two of them, an Englishman and a Dane, fell out. The Dane was a married man, and his behaviour where a girl was concerned might have had something to do with the bad feeling. The Englishman gave him a tumblerful of pure gin, and it nearly killed him. The fat was in the fire, and the Dane challenged him to a duel. He really meant it.

Now this sort of thing isn't supposed to go on at highbrow Oxford conferences. The Englishman was a man of some character, and because he was the person challenged, he had the right to choose the weapons. So boldly he said, 'Right, we'll fight it out at dawn tomorrow morning' (in the best tradition), 'and we'll fight it out with dusters!' The Dane was totally disgusted.

So I thought in terms of a duel – a spiritual duel. And the weapons of that warfare, I can assure you, are not dusters.

The Devil's Weapons

Revelation came gradually, and very often God's revelation does come gradually: if you got it all at once you could be overpowered by it and unable to retain it all. But it came in a very nice, gradual way. First of all there came 'Weapons that Satan uses' – weapons, and then conditions which become weapons in his hand. At first I thought we would take three of the devil's and three of the Christian's weapons. But the number grew and grew, because it was difficult to confine it to three. Ultimately I had it nice and even: seven apiece. Then when it was all neat and tidy, others kept occurring to me which were too important to omit.

Amongst the first group to occur were Deceit, Discouragement, Introspection and Self-pity. And then three conditions: Immorality, Occultism and Fear. From these conditions weapons are forged. We will take the various weapons in order.

Deceit

The first is **Deceit**: a weapon in the hand of the devil. He is a deceiver: a liar and the father of lies. Have you ever noticed how often you have been deceived? He tells you terrible lies, about yourself and about others. We have a wonderful facility to hear and to believe the voice of the

devil. He is very subtle, and he does not always face you
with a lie that is easily recognized as such. And so the
heading for this section is not 'Lying', but 'Deceit'. He
uses the lying mechanism to deceive you, and you find
that you are believing and acting on his lie. You pick up
an impression, or you overhear a remark that someone
has made, and it gets twisted and taken out of context,
often leading to bitterness and anger against the person
who is supposed to have said it. Sometimes it is only in
the afterward that you find there was a tremendous mis-
understanding: things weren't what they seemed at all. I
have been absolutely amazed at the devil's ability to
deceive – to deceive me (I am not talking only about other
folk). It happened very recently in a situation which
nobody knows anything about because I didn't say
anything (I have learned a little wisdom as I have grown
older). Something was really annoying me. I didn't think I
had any particular right to be annoyed, but you know how
you can be quite unreasonably so. In my case I could not
only have thought something unjust, but I could have
voiced my feeling. In the afterward I discovered the truth
of the situation. And I would have been absolutely morti-
fied if I had said one word, because the misjudgment was
almost total. Moreover, as it happened, if I had spoken
when I was so irritated, it would have been at a critical
point for the person concerned, and they could have taken
a wound that might have bled for a long, long time. I had
been deceived. The matter seemed one way, but it wasn't
that way at all.

I wonder how many of you believe that others think
such-and-such about you, feel such-and-such about you,
when in fact it is just not true? We are deceived again and
again. And because we think wrong things about each
other, there is many a church that is weak and powerless
and never makes the grade because the members internally
are feuding with each other, and they are listening to
carried stories. When you actually get to the heart of a
matter, very often you will find that 'there is so much

good in the worst of us, and so much bad in the best of us, that it ill becomes any of us to criticize the rest of us.' Often there is very little in these matters that a dose of the love of Christ cannot sort out. But the arch-deceiver is in: 'You know, she said such-and-such, and she thinks such-and-such, and his real attitude is such-and-such.' It stirs, and it stirs, and love goes out of the window as powerlessness comes in at the door, and Satan sets one against another. I say again: often when a matter is investigated, it is found to be based on deceit. How sure are you of the basis of the animosities that you are carrying in your deepest heart?

Always remember that as a deceiver the devil will feed you with lies, and we have a wonderful capacity to believe him. Always take this into consideration in your assessment of situations. '**Is** the devil in this? **Where** is he in it? What wrong impression may I be labouring under?' People have often come for counselling carrying fearfully wrong impressions of situations and people. Things were not as they thought at all. They had been deceived by that wicked one. He is a twister of truth. Christ knew how to handle him: *Get thee behind me, Satan*.

I realize there are many categories of deception, and I am not going to overtax you (or myself). But I want you to ponder for a moment. What lies may you be believing about other people now? Where you are judging people, are you quite sure of your judgment? Haven't you often found in the past that when things unfolded you were wrong to some degree? Does the devil have you in his grip, and is his deception working?

Discouragement

Have you ever noticed the number of depressing words that start with a **d**? I list a few of these for your consideration: deceit, despair, despondency, depression, dejection, desperation, degradation, damnation, destruction, dementia, defilement, defeat, dread – a whole pile of the Dreadful **D**s. And Satan uses that pile very regularly. From it he draws the second weapon that we shall consider: **Discouragement**.

I often refer to the weapon of discouragement. Someone once pictured an auction of the devil's weapons. I do not recollect the details accurately, or what all the other weapons were (I think lust, hatred and murder all figured); but there was one weapon at auction which I do recollect, and it was an ugly-looking, cross-grained implement; there was nothing attractive about it. It wasn't gold or silver or beautifully formed; it was base and ugly, distorted, nothing fetching about it. It was not the kind of thing you would have taken home and put on the mantelpiece. But though it was ungainly, it was very highly priced. An onlooker wondered about this and sought enlightenment.

'Ah,' the guide said, 'That is one of the devil's most valued weapons. That weapon is called discouragement.'

Ponder this. Have you ever been discouraged? Have you tried to do something for God and it hasn't worked? You have been working with lives, and instead of going on they have wilted under your hand, and gone back. And you say, 'What's the use? If that one went back, how can I ever trust anybody?' You become discouraged. Even at natural levels, in the business world, for example, a firm may be having a really rough time and ultimately the bosses become totally discouraged. And sometimes on to the scene comes fresh young blood that has never known discouragement, and the newcomer takes a grip on the situation and drives on to success. Discouragement is not on their horizon: they don't know anything about it. They haven't had the experience of going through a really bad time and being deeply affected.

Now, friends, discouragement is never of God. If things haven't worked out, learn from them. But keep in the front of your mind always that God is, and He is the rewarder of them that diligently seek Him (Hebrews 11:6). God is God, and the future is success and victory, it is not defeat. Remember the number of occasions when the ancestral line through which Christ came seemed to be in dire jeopardy, in danger of being broken again and again through the centuries – but it never did break. One thinks of Rahab the harlot; Ruth, widowed and childless; and David, confronting Goliath and later hunted by Saul. Danger, dire danger – but God. Always, **but God**. The scarlet thread never broke. And success was at the end of the story.

Never give way to discouragement. Use discouragement as a means of attaining a greater height. Say to God, 'All right. I failed. **You** didn't fail. Now let me have **Your** way of going about things.' Be fully and totally encouraged, and go on with God. There is no darkness or failure at the end of God's road, only at the end of the devil's road, and at the end of your road. All you need to do is to be on God's road. There your life will be blessed and a blessing. There is no defeat in Christ. There is no failure in Christ. You will succeed, I tell you: I say it absolutely and completely without reservation or modification. You will succeed, as Christ lives out His life in you. That way is open to us every one, and there are no favourites with God.

I am sympathetic to people who are discouraged. I feel for people who are discouraged. But, friend, it is a lie of the devil that you have been listening to. There is nothing negative in God; there is no discouragement in God. He is always an encourager. The Holy Spirit is an encourager. I don't care what pit you are in, I don't care how low you are; God's word to you is a word of encouragement. He doesn't say, 'Lie there.' He doesn't say, 'Go down lower.' He always says, 'Come up higher.' And He points to a cross where the remedy lies. There is a door that is open and a way that is open. Never give way to discouragement. You say, 'But wait. I really did try, and things didn't work out my way.' Is that not precisely the trouble? 'Your way' – you started at the wrong end. If, instead of trying to serve God and work for God and get things done

your way, you had let Him have **His** way, might you not have had more chance of success? If instead of doing things your way you had died to self, to ambition, even spiritual ambition, even the work-of-God ambition, and you had let the doctrine of death to self search you to the core, the way would have worked out because it would have been God's way, and His way never fails us; His way is always fruitful.

Now believe me. If you end your day as a failure, you will be judged for it. God will not sympathize with you or justify you. He will not say, 'You had a very hard time; I understand, and all is well.' **You will be judged and condemned because no son or daughter of Adam's race ever needs to end a failure.** I say that categorically, absolutely, without reservation. If you go down, you are a guilty sinner, and you will deserve the condemnation and the judgment that comes upon you at the end of the day. You don't have to go down, and if you do, it will be an evidence of a rebellious wilfulness in you to get your own way. We never need to fail, and if we do we will get in the end what we richly deserve.

M'm. Never thought of failure as a sin? Well, get it into the sin category right now. It is a sin to fail.

I think I am managing to stir some of the sleepiness out of the bones of my audience, and some of you are beginning to say, 'I don't know that I agree with that.' I reply: if you tell me you are justified in failing, you are telling me that Christ is not able to uphold you. I don't know how you will maintain that. Christ cannot fail, and discouragement should be resisted.

Friends, over the years I have found Christ work mighty miracles and make wonderful provision – souls saved, demons cast out, sick folks healed, finance provided for many buildings. I tell you that if I was starting life again I would believe for more. Never be discouraged. All you need to do is get on to God's path. Your own will never work out. Be like Hudson Taylor. He maintained that if God gives a promise it will always work, and if it doesn't work never doubt God but look inside to see what's wrong. Did you mistake guidance? Did you go out on your own? Had you a wrong motive deep down somewhere? Go with God, let Him lead, and there will be a fulfilment of those things that are spoken: always. His word never falls to the ground. Let me encourage you, friends. Oh, the door is so wide open and the world is so large, there is work for all of us. We don't need to get in each other's way, we don't need to be crossing each other's paths in competition. The world is wide and the needs are mighty. Get on to God's lines. I would encourage you. Discouragement is a weapon of the devil.

Introspection

As we come to one of the devil's crowning glories, there are some learned professors of **Introspection** right here under my nose. Some of you are experts on it, and I must confess that I was once a prince of introspection. You could have told me nothing about introspection that I didn't know. I was a wonderful introspector. I sometimes listen to Susie giving testimony: she says that she worried about everything and she worried about nothing, but one thing she did: she worried.[2] And one thing I did was, I introspected. I would go over what I had done and why I had done it, and would it have been better if I hadn't done this or that? You go over matters long dead and they bind and grip you.

This is a fearful weapon. With it the devil pulls souls down desperately and viciously. I want to go into this carefully and not just rush over the headings. I really want to try to help people here.

Introspection is 'looking into me'. It often involves concentrating on areas of problem, areas of difficulty. And the more we concentrate on them, the worse they get. I am often reminded of a cyclist. A big stone or pothole in the middle of the road fascinates, indeed almost hypnotizes, him. It is amazing how often he either hits the stone or goes into the pothole. He does so because it focuses his attention on itself and draws like a magnet. If he could but say, 'That's over there in the middle: I'm not going there,' and get his eye on something on the side, he could evade it. But he gets his eye on it and he goes down. And you too go down and down as you get your eye on your troubles.

You may say, 'Now, wait a minute. This isn't reasonable. If there is something wrong in me, I'll have to have a look at it.'

Did it ever do you any good having a look at it? I'll tell you what you do need to do. You need to have a situation opened up. The Holy Spirit Himself will touch situations and He will draw your attention to them, but He does not want you to focus your attention on them for ever after. He wants you to be aware of them and to have them dealt with, normally within a few moments of the revelation – not six years after you have been going over and over them. You can be like a dog with a bone. You will not let it go. You are looking in and in and in. You will find that this vocabulary comes to you: **I, me, my, mine; my problem; this happened to me; I've got to look in to see how I am getting on inside.** It is a total focusing of attention on yourself and the areas of difficulty. I have never met a soul in all my life who found liberation this way.

You say, 'Oh, well, I'll need to pray and fast about it. I'll need to set days aside in prayer.' If you do, the latter condition is liable to be worse than the first, because instead of simply taking a glimpse at the position and handing the matter over to Christ, you get down on your knees and you pray about it. Your door is locked, and you focus on the problem; you focus on it for hours, and you say, 'O God, the miserable sinner that I am! O God, You know this problem. O God, take this problem away!' You are gazing at it and gazing at it, and it is getting worse and worse.

Never do that. There is no future in it. That is not how God lifts you; it is not how God deepens spiritual life. Never do it. You say, 'But wait a minute. I know this thing is wrong, and I want to make sure I get it out by the roots.' Thus you concentrate on it. Thus you say, 'I must pray about it.'

I know I have already referred to this, but I want to emphasize it again.

I challenge you. Is there any one of you who ever heard me tell you to go and pray about your problem? Ever? Never! **Never pray about it!** It is a very dangerous thing to pray about it. When you do so, you focus attention on it. God says, 'Let it alone – drop it into the sea of My forgetfulness. Let it be covered by the blood of Christ, to be remembered no more for ever.' You don't pray **into** a problem: you pray **out** of it. You praise God for the deliverance that there is in Jesus. Never introspect about anything all the days of your life. Listen and reach out – get the revelation of God. When you have got that, leave your troubles with God, and never think about them again.

There is one thing that characterized Hudson Taylor, that mighty man of God. He would make a decision as he felt led under God, and he never again looked over his shoulder to ask if it was right. He made decisions in honesty before God, and then neither hell nor high water blew him off course. There was stability, resolution, determination, character, iron grip and strength.

Never be tempted with introspection. The devil will use it and he will ruin your life with it. There are people who have been through hell again and again. Some come to me on the phone from time to time with troubles stemming from introspection. I want to speak kindly and not to say anything that will put any of you off phoning me, because I will always try to help you. But you will never find me telling you to go and think or pray about your problem. You will find me telling you to leave it behind you and take the victory in Christ that is for you now, absolutely and completely. And I do not want you merely to say, 'Ah, yes, that's a good idea, yes, I understand that.' I want you to put it in practice. Make a resolution inside yourself to **do** it, to drop introspection totally. Have one honest look, get the revelation of God, and pass on into victory.

As I said, I am an expert on introspection. I speak with authority on this. I was one of the greatest introspectors in the world, and I still have to keep a grip on it. I am being honest and true – I still have to watch introspection. There is a chapter in Finney, in a remarkable series of lectures on revival, in which he encourages readers to investigate their sins of commission and omission. (He was preaching in America, where there was a great deal of very slack living, and he was bringing sin sharply to the attention of people.) I have been careful for most of a lifetime about whom I recommend that chapter to – because it can be dangerously binding. It has a funny side too, or perhaps I should say some of the reactions to the chapter can be funny. Finney tells you to go down the list and write out a catalogue of the sins of omission of which you are guilty. He says that as you do this other sins will come to mind. Go over the list again, and more and more sins will come to mind that you have long forgotten. And when you are finally through the first list of sins of omission, you have to compile the list of sins of commission. To get through the latter is very difficult, but what shall I say of the former? When I first met it I found it mind-boggling. And yet the whole exercise has its funny side. You will start off, maybe, with a sheet of paper, and you end up with pages of foolscap!

I found that the exercise had a fearfully binding effect on me, a truly terrible effect. It so tied me up that I lost the sense of the presence of God – to such an extent that Miss Taylor almost got to the point of despairing totally that I would ever make the grade spiritually. Now this was because of introspection over-indulged. It was as bad as that. And I teach this now, friends. Go and be honest with God. Any sin the Holy Spirit brings before you, get rid of it through the blood of Christ. But don't go eternally digging into the past for every little mistake you ever made.

There are family traits, and I think you can inherit a bit of this. My daughter Mary was once an introspector as well, and she is also a logician; her degree is in philosophy. Mary could take a situation and develop it logically. You couldn't touch the logic of it. But often she ended up with something that was a total nonsense, because her reasoning started from a wrong premise. The basis was wrong; there was an error at the bottom, and as a result the conclusion was wrong. She had inherited, I think largely from me, a tendency to introspect. You must watch that kind of thing if it lies in your nature. I can now stand outside situations and be objective, knowing how vulnerable I once was. I tell you, introspection can be a hellish weapon in the hand of the devil. And I am sure many of you will agree with that. It can ruin a person's whole life. Your whole spiritual life can be shattered by introspection. So if you are ever tempted to go alone, to pray about a problem, be careful. Go to God for the revelation of a solution. Look upward and never downward, outward and never inward. The Holy Spirit will reveal to you all you need to know about the inwardness. You don't need to go and dig things up. Forgiven sin is under the blood; it has been put away. But you have perhaps been in a very intense meeting where your old sin has been highlighted. Maybe Achan has been mentioned, and you wonder, 'Is everything all right?' You go and dig up the thing that was long buried, just the way a dog does. Indeed in counselling people I often illustrate this subject with reference to dogs. You know what a dog does when it finds an old bone it buried long ago: it rolls on it. I don't know why, but roll it does. Then it must come into the house to share the smell. We all get the benefit of it, and it's awful.

Now that is what you do in the spiritual world. You get hold of an old bone. You get hold of an old sin that was formerly brought to the light and put away. You begin to think about it again, bringing it back to the surface of your mind. Maybe it's not totally away; maybe there's something still there. Maybe there's a memory that has to be cleansed. Maybe ... maybe... You roll on it, and you are positively spiritually smelly when you come to me or to some other counsellor with something that ought never to have been raised again. So if from time to time I just comment to you, 'You're a bit whiffy today,' you will know what I mean!

On the other hand there are some of you who are differently built. Introspection doesn't touch you, it never has touched you. You are as free as birds. But, friends, watch that you are not carelessly letting unforgiven sin lie hidden under the carpet of your life. There is a balance. You have got to let the Holy Spirit examine everything. But when He has dealt with sin, be rid of it and the memory of it, and rejoice in the freedom of the sons of God.

Resist the devil. He would tie you up in introspection; he would ruin your life through introspection.

Self-Pity

Here is a beauty: **Self-pity**. I can catch your response, as you rise like the trout to the fly! Who? me? Poor me! Self-pity: I wonder if there is any one of us who doesn't have any of it in us at all. It is deadly; absolutely deadly is self-pity.

Now, come on. How many of you are caught on self-pity? 'What he did to me. What she did to me. What the minister said and he shouldn't have said, and how unjustly I've been treated. And I'm really quite sorry for myself, I'm not getting a fair deal, and I really never have had a fair deal. My gifts are not recognized, and people are unkind.' I think self-pity is one of the most pitiable things from which Christians suffer. I have no respect for it. It is a totally useless emotion to indulge.

I am going to tell you a story – a very important story, you understand! I might have been killed!

See me there: just a bit of a boy, sent out with provisions for the farm workers in the fields; it was often a boy's job to do that. Very nasty things were said about me as a tea-carrier, for I hated the job. I went with very reluctant feet, and evidently the hopeful tea-drinkers used to joke amongst themselves:

'Is that a post?'

'No, I don't think so. It's moving.'

'It's not moving very much. And the tea will be getting cold.'

Little I cared whether the tea was cold or not; it was not I who was drinking it, and I didn't want to be there in the first place.

On the occasion in question I had gone with the tea, and it was a far distance: a long, long walk for a wee boy.

This was shortly before I had learned to ride on horseback. And there was a big black pony – hack, really – that the workers were sending back because they were finished with it for the day. After they had drunk their tea they said, 'You take the pony back.' They chucked me up on its back, although I could not ride, and off I went. The pony still had all its working harness on. Now horses are a bit like ourselves. This one knew it was going home, and it knew that food was associated with home. So it went with quite evident anticipation, and the road it travelled was mighty rough (it still is, as you will see if you ever go there). The animal moved from walking to trotting, and I can tell you that trotting is difficult for a person who cannot ride. Galloping, which is faster, is actually easier: the horse's legs are then moving in pairs. But in trotting the legs are not moving in this kind of unison – and you are up and down and up and down. As black pony thought more and more about its corn it went faster and faster. And off its back I went. As I fell, my foot became entangled in the harness and I was dragged at the tail of a runaway horse, like Annas' son who met his death that way in Jerusalem. I was carried upside down, my back and head bumping along on the rocky road.

To say I was sorry for myself is a mighty understatement. I positively wallowed in self-pity. Ultimately, it may have been by an action of God – I certainly don't think it was an action of the devil – my foot got disentangled. Black pony went on at high speed, and I was left lying there on a very hard road. Like Jonah, I was exceedingly sorry for myself and felt I was justified in being sorry for myself. This had happened to poor me. My precious head had been hitting big rocks. There I lay moaning and groaning inwardly, if not outwardly. I tend not to give way to much outward expression. Such behaviour would not have been manly. But oh, I was exceedingly sorry for myself. I was full of self-pity. But after about ten or fifteen minutes realization dawned: 'This is a pretty grim place to lie! Nobody sees me, and nobody is sorry for me. In fact nobody is particularly aware of my existence. I could be left lying here for hours, and there's no future at all in staying here; I may as well get up.' Mummy's boy was getting nothing out of the situation. So I got to my knees and on to my feet, and I made my limping way home.

In one moment of time I realized how foolish and pointless self-pity was. It had no future, no future at all. I did not realize it then, but I passed a critical point that day. I think never again did I seriously indulge self-pity.

Never indulge it. If you do, you will be in danger of ultimately disgusting your friends. They will be very kind and nice at first. But afterwards, although they may never say a word to you, they will brand you as a self-pitier, and they will only listen to the beginning of the moans and groans and injustices before switching off. There was one lady I used to know who was unique in this way. When you met her in the street, she would start by saying, 'How are you?' and before you could answer she would go on: 'You know, I'm not well at all.' And she would go through a dozen diseases, one after another – and this every time you met her. It got worse and worse. On one occasion she even got me to send her hat to a policeman friend for analysis. She suspected that somebody had put some kind of powder in it to cause a skin trouble. There was, of course, no such thing there. It was ordinary dandruff! Resist self-pity. The devil can get it into your mind that you are the most ill-done-to person in the world, and it's a lie. I have to counsel much on this. Sometimes a person will be thinking that their cross is the heaviest in the whole church. I tell you, in some of our gatherings I can look around and pick out half-a-dozen people who think the same thing. They cannot all be right, but since they don't know the details of each other's cases they misjudge – and if such details were revealed many a person would be astonished.

Get rid of self-pity. It is not healthy. It does not make for spiritual growth. It is a totally useless emotion. View it as a spiritual cancer and a strong weapon in the hand of the devil.

Immorality

The fifth weapon is of a different type, but I feel I should include it here. It is **Immorality**.

Now you object, 'Immorality is not a weapon, but a condition.'

In the hand of the devil the condition becomes a weapon. He deliberately brings immorality before people, and they look, and are entrapped in the looking. This is serious. There are very few people who come to us for counsel who are not affected by immorality to some degree. Now I don't mean that they are all guilty of adultery or fornication – although you do get both of these. But very many of them have indulged at some time or other in irregular sex (sex without marriage), and it has left its mark. Many have been involved in reading literature that is unclean. An increasing number have become involved in pornography, not always wilfully, but it has happened. Television has had a deeply defiling influence. You can hardly pick up a normal newspaper today without finding smut. All of these things coming against the human spirit cause a reaction, and they are all associated with immorality. Often a person is simply curious to know. Don't allow that curiosity to have its way. Eve was curious ... she wanted to know. The day came when she did know. She should never have known anything about evil, but the day came when she knew good and evil. We were never meant to know evil: never.

But evil is dangled under our noses. I will tell you how it works. We are all born with natural instincts. Therefore there is an interest in things of a sexual nature in a perfectly normal, natural way. But the devil comes in on that which is normal and natural and he brings his own lurid fascination by presenting something that is not legitimate, something that is not in the will of God. And in our curiosity we follow after – 'I wonder what it is like. I'd like to read a bit more about this. I'd like to see some of this sort of stuff that you read about in the papers, pornography: what is it all about?' You are watching television. And I know what happens. Although I don't have television, I have been present where it has been on. I remember in one case I went to see a man who was roughcasting one of our churches. He was watching his set, and in courtesy I said, 'Don't worry, finish your programme. I'll talk to you when it ends.' There we both sat watching. It was perfectly innocent-looking. And then suddenly, without warning, in a moment of time it passed from being a reasonable programme to being a filthy programme. There is no other word I can use for it: it was filthy. Now I hope I don't tend to be self-righteous; I'm not built that way. But I suddenly thought, 'I can't stay here.' Apart from the deeper moral issue, I could not have anyone witness me looking at that programme. I said, 'I'll come back and talk to you about the business later.'

I once heard of a group of ministers who were together in a hotel watching television some years ago. One of them was a man much used of God. They were all watching. I don't know how bad it became. It might have been very mild; I don't know. But he had the courage to stand up and say, 'Look, gentlemen. You may be able to watch this kind of thing without danger, but I'm not. I'm going.' That man was used in powerful evangelism across the nation, a name that is honoured, a man that God used. I don't even know the names of any other one of them. Maybe that is not without significance. Holiness unto the Lord – let it be 'our watchword and song'.

What I now say may shock some of you, but there is no way round this. In deliverance ministry there is an opening up of that which is normally covered. We all wear masks – and thank God we do wear masks; otherwise we couldn't stand what we should see. As people come in great need and in the grip of demon power, they are often so desperate that they open up. And the uncovering can be fearful. Also, please believe me when I say that very many young people who are coming into the churches today need deliverance because they have been in such deep pollution. The scene is very different from forty years ago.

Recently I took a conference in London at which I had asked Diana Rutherford, who is very deeply used in this line of ministry, to speak near the end.[3] She indicated a number of conditions that she had discerned, and she said, 'One of the things that is coming through to me most powerfully in this meeting is immorality, and particularly immorality amongst men.' And she was absolutely correct. She discerned a chronic condition.

You say, 'What do you mean?'

I don't mean that a great number of men are in adulterous relationships. I don't mean that most men are living immoral lives in the deep sense of that word. But the number of people who are troubled with immoral thoughts, with fantasy, with the effects of things that they have seen on television or in the press, is very great. Pornography has touched many, and there is an inner soiling. One of the main ways in which the devil gets in amongst people, is through immorality.

Now let me make a clear statement. God is against everything of a perverted nature in sex. The do-gooders can tell you that homosexuality is all right, and lesbianism is not a sin. I know that people can have a tendency in these directions, and the tendency isn't a sin, but acting on it is. And the Bible is totally against all forms of immorality, all illicit sex, sex without marriage. We are in a permissive society, and the world says, 'It is perfectly all right.' God says it is totally wrong. The law of God never changes from generation to generation.

Immorality has always been a fearful power in the hands of the devil to whip men and women. Many are troubled at night in their dream life. They are troubled in their subconscious thought life. Many are good men, and they have pushed these evil things down, where they have suppurated down in the subconscious realm.

I remember one case. A godly young man came into one of our gatherings, and he was so pleased at the general quality of the meeting – you could see him nodding his head in agreement from time to time. I suddenly touched on deliverance, and his head went down as though he had been pole-axed. He told me later that as a boy his father had pretended to strangle him, and for ever after there was something like a collar round his neck choking him, and nobody could ever get near to touching that collar, that spiritual thing. He couldn't let anyone near his neck – not even his own wife in bed at night. And in the very midst of the meeting it dropped off and he was free, but he came for ministry afterwards and he said, 'Look, before I was converted I was involved in a particular type of sin and the effects of it are still with me.' God delivered him that night. He goes right down to the bottom of the pollutions that have troubled us, where they have been pushed down into the subconscious, and He sets us free.

Purity

Although I am keeping the weapons of the devil and the weapons of God in two separate compartments, I want to jump across the barrier for a moment from the devil's weapon of Immorality to God's weapon of Purity.

Purity is linked with power; purity **is** power. If you ever want to be powerful for God, you will have to be pure – not just in the outer circumference of life, but in the heart.

Let me illustrate this from alcoholism. An ex-alcoholic or ex-drinker passing the pub feels all that old desire drawing him back in. But he says, 'No, I'm not going in,' and he continues past the pub and comes to another: 'Oh, I'm drawn – but no, I'm not going in.' That is not God's way, in the last analysis. Although it is better than going back in, God ultimately goes to the bottom of the problem and He takes the wretched alcoholism out of His child. Now the only way the ex-addict is going into the pub is to preach to the people in it. There is no longer a draw of alcohol: he has been set free at the deepest depths. There are many men and women who want to live aright, and God understands that. But often deep down they are full of lust. They are not going to follow the lust, but they have it. And Jesus in his wonderful and incisive way puts His hand on it.

> *Thou shalt not commit adultery: But I say unto you, that every one that looketh on a woman to lust after her hath committed adultery with her already in his heart.* (Matthew 5:27–8)

It is not only the outside of you that Christ cleans up; it is the inside of you as well. It is the heart. Purity is power, and you will never have full power without purity in the heart.

It is not enough in the law of God that you don't commit adultery. God takes you to a place where you don't feel adulterous. He goes right down to the very bottom of your being, to cleanse until there is a purity that is a positive, shining glory. And I tell you, in the war with Satan it is of tremendous significance that you carry with you the purity of Jesus. You carry with you the power of Jesus if you carry with you the purity of Jesus. If there is any touch of immorality in any life, bring it to Christ. Don't push it down. Say, 'Lord, open me up.' Open it up, let it up and out, as the hand of Christ touches and the blood of Christ cleanses. God wants you free at the deepest level. When I preach on deliverance, people so often think of the negative side. Deliverance **out of** binding evil. I tell you, one of the glories of deliverance is positive: emancipation **into** the fullness of the life of Christ. It is not just out of bondage: it is into freedom. He came that we might have life and that we might have it abundantly. Blessed be the name of the Lord.

Perhaps I should relate one incident from which we may learn a salutary lesson. An outstandingly clean person, knowing almost nothing about the unclean side of life but being inquisitive, had read one pornographic book. That individual had to come for deliverance from demon power. One book! You have no idea of the power of immorality. I have known a person come for deliverance and be delivered, and be repossessed before they were out of the door, by deliberately indulging unclean thoughts. 'Oh,' you say, 'I thought repossession would have involved action.' That, my friend, **is** action: a deliberate turning back at a mental level can give re-entrance in moments of time. You are up against a powerful weapon in the hand of the devil when you are dealing in the realm of immorality.

You may think I am exaggerating. It is not so, not by a hairbreadth. You have no idea of the danger of even the fine shades of immorality. Every movement towards perversion, every movement towards irregularity in the sex life, anything that cannot be seen under the blazing eyes of Christ, is out. That's it: that is the standard. If Christ is not with you in the activity, it is out. Totally, completely, and for ever, without reservation or a back door open to bring it back. Nothing should ever happen that would not happen with the known presence of the Lord Jesus right there. And of course He is right there.

Occultism

The sixth of the enemy's weapons is **Occultism** – another condition that becomes a weapon. Again, forty years ago we seldom met it. But nowadays it is amazing how many people in churches have been involved in occultism at some level or other. Quite amazing – and quite horrific, actually. There is a peculiar fascination in the occult that can trap spiritually-minded people before they know very much about God. They may be aware of a spiritual dimension and have no church connection, or be in a comparatively dead church where there is not much of a strong spiritual nature being experienced. They feel, however, that there **is** a world out there. They hear things, they read books, and they become convinced that there is at least a world of evil. They are not very sure about the world of God.

I remember something that happened to me as a young Christian; I would be about sixteen at the time. I came from a background which was Christian but not really very deeply spiritual. I was on holiday with an aunt and cousins in Edinburgh. On one particular day, left to amuse myself, I wandered into a library. There I met a young teacher who was a very sociable fellow, and we started chatting. We got on to the subject of the occult. He probably led the conversation that way. Demonism and demonology came up. He said, 'I'll show you where there are books about it.' He then introduced me to the section of the library where they were stacked. I found in these books an area that I had never explored and knew nothing about. It was completely new, and I wanted to know more. So I read deeply about demonology. There were fantastic and horrible things in that book. But full of the pride of youth, I read on – 'It will not do **me** any harm. I can think for myself,' and so on. I ultimately got home, had a normal evening, and went to bed.

There was a bedside light, and as I switched it off the filament was imprinted on my inner vision. But then shapes and images began to form around it. The world of evil and of the occult suddenly blazed before my eyes, and I could not shut it out. I was being invaded. For the first time in my life my mind was being compelled from outside, beyond my control. I suppose I cried on God from my deepest being, because I felt myself going down into the horrors of hell. And God rescued me. I regained control and was able to shut the images out. And never from that hour to this has that world had any such power. It was a miracle of God that drew me up.

Now I had not been wanting to go into that world. I had merely been intellectually curious. I had no intention of being anywhere near demons – though I do realize, now that I look back, that there was held out to me in a peculiar way the feeling, 'You can get power. There is a road of power here.' I had a background from which there was really no chance of my going that way: but think of an experience like this coming to people with no such background. In my case it was frightening, not fascinating. But there is a lure, a weird fascination for many, in the dark arts: in witchcraft for instance. The occult draws powerfully. Christ could say, *'I, if I be lifted up, will draw all men unto Me.'* While there is a magnetism of heaven, there is also a magnetism of evil – a magnetism of hell. Today this kind of evil is swamping America and coming increasingly to this country. It has been reckoned that there are about 50,000 children sacrificed to the devil in America every year, and that same pattern is developing in Britain, though on a smaller scale. It is alleged that children are being sacrificed; they are being ritually killed. And women are kept to become, as they call them, brood mares. Their progeny is never registered; they are born to be sacrificed, born to be killed. This, in Britain today.[4]

Separate yourself totally from the occult. When the breath of it touches you, you will be defiled. Whether it was the ouija board you were indulging in, tarot cards, or any other form of the occult, you have to be cleansed.

In this particular line of ministry in our midst it is largely Diana and Grace who are used.[5] There are things that they don't speak much about. I have known Grace meet a demon in her spirit and fight with it for days, perhaps before a conference, until the person in whom it is, appears. Then it surfaces and is cast out by the power of God: it is known, seen, recognized. I often tell of the occasion when, just before calling people out for ministry, I asked Diana to say a little about her experiences in dealing with demons. The story has a humorous side to it – I am well able, as most of you know, to upset most congregations if I am going full tilt on this subject, and I don't really need any help from Diana to cause consternation. But there she stood and, bland as butter, said, 'Oh, yes, I can see demons. I can see them as I am walking along the street. I can see where they are in this hall right now. A woman went out about ten minutes ago, and it was a demon of rebellion that took her out.' There were about 200 in that audience. When the opportunity came, about 120 of them sought help for many different needs. I do not for a moment suggest that they all had demons, but there were many demons there. Indeed, I will never forget a terrible feeling of evil in the background of that city. I heard on that night confession of sin that I have never heard anywhere else at any time. Some of it I don't know that I have ever revealed to anyone, even amongst those who are working most closely with me in this ministry.

I wonder how far I dare shock you. Are you strong enough to bear the revelation of what is ongoing right now? I will take two cases.

A Haunted House

The first involves a haunted house. The lady who lived alone in it was a **very** level-headed and controlled person – not at all neurotic or fanciful – but by the time she sought help she had been driven almost crazy by the horrors attending the haunting. I will not go into all the weird happenings, but they were horrific. Things had reached a stage where she had been assaulted by an entity.

I went with Diana and Grace to see her and, as so often happens in such circumstances when there is a real haunting, I felt ice coldness coming over me. We prayed, and I felt my part was done. Something critical broke, but it became obvious that there was more to follow. Grace and Diana took charge of the next part. In her spirit Grace had seen the entity days before this. Diana perceived it in animal form – like a horrible wolf. I will leave Diana and Grace to tell their own stories. Tell, Diana, of the power of the blood.

This was my first experience of dealing with haunted houses, and I didn't quite know what to expect!

It was an older lady who occupied the house. She had been tormented for months and was literally petrified. She was beginning to think she was going out of her mind with her experiences, and had no idea that this type of thing was not uncommon.

We arrived at the house, and Mr Black asked to be shown where the manifestations had taken place. We were taken into the bedroom.

I was not looking for any physical indication of a presence, but almost immediately was left with a sense of coldness, like cold fingers touching my face. We prayed as a group, Mr Black leading in prayer, and almost immediately the coldness left. Grace and I were then asked to lead in prayer, which we did, but both of us were left with an uneasy feeling.

Over a cup of tea afterwards, the two of us discussed privately our inner spiritual feelings, to discover they were mutual, and so Grace and I returned to the bedroom to pray further.

This time, alone, the anointing and power of the Holy Spirit fell on us and I saw clearly an evil beast-type creature in the room. I always feel in such circumstances the urge to face it, to look at it. As I did that, I found that it couldn't look at me – it couldn't look at Christ within me; it wasn't really interested in me at all. I was very aware of it standing behind me to my right. It was trying to hide. As we prayed, the blood of Christ came like a shield between me and the entity, and I felt a tremendous power. I'd had a horrible feeling all down my back as if the thing was so close that it was almost touching me. As the blood of Christ came, there was a feeling of total covering. It was as though the blood became a shield, and I used that shield to drive the entity back, under the power of the Holy Spirit. As I lifted that shield again and again in the face of the beast, it turned and ran, snarling, terrified. Its whole face became one of fear and absolute terror: it could no longer stand before the presence of the blood of Christ. It was glorious to see the work of the devil defeated through the power of the blood, and to know its wonderful protection.

We then sat quietly in the room until it began to fill with the presence of Christ as He came and made His residence there. Gradually the atmosphere became 'thick' with His glory. It reminded me of times I have seen the very atmosphere in church meetings change. It is as though the natural light begins to fill with a supernatural light. Sometimes it has become so intense that I can scarcely see through it. That happened on this occasion; it was wonderful.

Our final test was that we knew we would both be perfectly happy to sleep in that room alone at night, such was the sense of peace around us.

I left feeling very contented with my first experience of a haunted house. It was with some dismay that we received a phone call, I think about two weeks later. The manifestations had started again, and this time they were worse!

A little confused, we returned to the house to try and get to the root of the problem. Indeed I sensed in my spirit that all was not well; I could feel the darkness coming around me before I got to the house.

Grace and I asked to be alone in the bedroom immediately. As we chatted and opened ourselves for revelation, we became very aware of a deep need within the lady of the house herself. I had in fact been aware of this need the first time we met there, but as we had been asked to pray over the house I had not opened myself to deal with that side of things as well.

We asked the lady to come through to the bedroom and began to probe a little into her past. She had been involved in things that certainly left big question marks in our minds, and we both felt very strongly that she needed deliverance from an evil entity. We prayed together and within a very short time an entity came rushing out of her screaming. It was a wonderful victory. It was good to get right down to the root of the matter. The lady herself, who had never experienced anything like that in her life, was delighted: I just remember her joy in being set free.

Alone again, we prayed over the room until the darkness departed and the light returned, knowing that this time things were complete.

That situation has remained clear. We last heard from the lady a few months ago, and she is still very grateful for all the help she received.

Grace's comments show how discernment operated even before events broke surface:

Word came to us of a lady who was very frightened when in her own house, especially at night. She was a Christian and very open to the suggestion that we go to her flat to pray. Before going, I encountered something dark in the spiritual world and knew that was the presence I would find there. Ultimately two of us were left alone in the room where the lady felt particularly troubled. We got down on our knees and there the evil was confronted and departed from the house as the light of Christ came. It was a high-rise block, and I remember going down the stairs and looking around in case it had not left the building, only the house.

About a week later I was wakened out of my sleep to the sound of that same presence bouncing beside my bed. I was not sure if the sound had been in my dreams, but the presence was certainly there. We discovered that the lady had found her house clear, but the trouble had returned. This time we questioned her, as we suspected that apart from any outside presence she herself needed deliverance. This she received, very wonderfully, and we felt that what had been in her had been acting as a magnet for the other, which had presumably remained inside the building. Two of us prayed again for the house. It was a much harder fight this time. The presence became a lingering darkness, but was ultimately expelled, and I felt this time that it was sent to the lake of fire. The lady was very grateful that God had so helped her.

There were actually three stages in the incident. After the entity was first dealt with it returned and it became evident that not only had the house needed cleansing but the lady herself required deliverance. After this happened, the work was soon completed. There was, however, an interesting aftermath. Diana had sought to make sure that the lady would be no more troubled, or the house re-entered – even if she had to face counter-attack herself. And indeed the evil thing did follow her for some days after. At that time there was not such clear knowledge as there is now of the authority under God to banish an entity to the pit, or wherever God indicates – although Grace did seem to get the beginning of revelation on the matter. We did, of course, all know of the possibility; but there is a great difference between using words of banishment and having the authority to do so and find the thing actually happening.

Another Haunting

In the second case, I had a phone call from a priest about a very disturbing haunting. A mother and her son of about six lived together and the boy spoke of a spirit child who often came to him. He was quite disturbed by events and in no way welcomed them. Evidently there had been tragedy in a house nearby where three children had been burned to death. There was also talk of a cot death nearby. The condition of affairs was described as desperate, and there was a real call for help.

I arranged to meet Grace and Diana on a particular day, but early on that morning, before leaving, a TV network was on the phone. They had heard of our plans and wished to be present to televise proceedings. I was not prepared to allow them to be involved. As it happened, it was not the lady of the house but a neighbour who had made contact, and we had no further difficulty.

And so we gathered – the lady and her six-year-old son, the priest, Diana, Grace and myself. The mother and lad told their stories and the impression was conveyed of a spirit child haunting the house, being visible to the boy, who was unhappy about the appearances and indeed in fear of them. I left the direction of matters with Grace and Diana, who chose to go alone into an upstairs room which was the most haunted part of the house. Meantime I chatted to the others downstairs. For the mother I was sorry; for the boy, who had a very gentle nature, there was real compassion. In due time Diana and Grace returned and later gave me a report.

In that upstairs room they met no gentle spirit of a dead child, but a horrible entity. They felt encompassed by a fog and opposed by a power which attempted to cause a break between them. After a protracted and bitter fight they had the victory and the entity was expelled. It was most reluctant to go – but finally it was compelled to leave.

Word came a week or two later that all was well in the house. There were no further manifestations.

I have asked Diana to supply her recollection of these events:

> We were asked to deal with another case of haunting in Helensburgh. It was of a little boy who was seeing 'another child' in his room at night, and he had become very frightened. The mother had a Catholic background and her priest had tried to help, but things had not changed, and so she contacted Mr Black.
>
> Mr Black, Grace and I went to the house and we felt a tremendous love and compassion for the little boy. He was only six or seven years old, and I could see the fear in his eyes as Mr Black asked him some simple questions. You could tell he wasn't making it up.
>
> Grace and I went upstairs to the bedroom and I was left alone for a few minutes. Almost immediately a fear tried to touch my spirit – a spine-chilling sensation that comes when you sense something else is in the room beside you! This was no 'child' that we sensed. It was an evil spirit, a very dark presence that perhaps had masqueraded as a 'child' to the little boy. What cruel tricks the enemy plays.
>
> We chatted quietly for a few minutes, then turned to prayer. The next thing that happened was a most odd sensation. I don't think I have ever felt it before or since. It was as though a mist began to fill the room. Grace was kneeling at one bed, and I at the other. For an awful moment, it seemed as if we were miles apart, or as if a great mist was blocking our spiritual link. I got up and moved closer, and together under that wonderful anointing that comes from on high we fought the powers of darkness until the mist began to break.
>
> The precious blood came again surrounding the room and the home, until Christ Himself came. We met with that One who always has time for children,

that One who has never shunned a child's prayer or cry for help.

The family (I think) were unsaved, and yet I do believe that because a child was frightened, because a child prayed, Christ came to help and comfort.

It was very sweet at the end. We were able to tell the mother quite confidently that we thought there would be no more bother. It was a joy to see a strained mother's face relax at the hope that this time her little boy would be tormented no more.

Mr Black prayed with the child at the end and the little boy snuggled into him as if he knew now that he was safe. He looked very contented.

We heard nothing from the family for several weeks, but eventually news reached us that all was well. What a joy to know that Christ cares for every child, every mother and every soul!

Grace adds additional details:

The troubled boy kept seeing a small child sitting at the end of his bed, waving to him and trying to communicate with him. Moreover the dog, a Rottweiler, would not go upstairs in the house. Animals can be very sensitive to the spiritual world (cf. Balaam's ass).

On this occasion I did not know what I would meet. I think perhaps I thought it might be a spirit masquerading as a child, but when we prayed I found it was no child spirit; it was a wickedness of darkness that is totally inhuman. Christ's compassion for that little child was wonderful. He came in and totally expelled the darkness. I found no liberty to pray for the whole building (it was an apartment in a block), but sensed as though a band of the blood of Christ came round that particular house to protect it. Some weeks later the mother phoned Mr Black to say that the boy was fine and there had been no further visitations. Christ does love the little children.

Let there be a complete separation from the occult in all its forms and a facing of the devil in the power of Christ. For those called to the ministry there is a total covering and there should be no fear. Jesus Christ is Lord.

Fear

The seventh weapon that I have listed is, you might have thought, a very simple one that I would have put higher up. But in fact it is not as simple as it seems. It is **Fear**. Many of you are well acquainted with fear in the phobic sense, because you have heard testimonies to that and it has been explained, and I will not take time here to go further into the phobic side.[6] But there are other fears, and there can be a danger of preachers thinking that everyone is like themselves. We know our own weaknesses, and in preaching can point out much about them, because we know how they work. We can often understand and explain them if they are constantly with us. But quite often fear is not included because most anointed preachers have got rid of it. Thus we tend to forget its power over others.

This takes me back to a night not long after my baptism in the Spirit. There was a small group of us meeting in a private house. Miss Taylor was present. These could be wonderful meetings. There was often a great anointing on Miss Taylor. She received tremendous depth of revelation, and you knew God was looking into you when she ministered. I remember kneeling at the opposite side of the room from her. We were all on our knees (we tended to be on our knees in those days more than we are now). She began to prophesy in a way that identified me. As she prophesied, a mantle fell over my head and shoulders. I could feel it, like a substantial cloak. As the prophecy went on, I had a remarkable experience. I suppose I was in a sense commissioned for a particular ministry that night, and suddenly I found that fear that I had never known was in me drained away. I honestly did not know until it went that it had been there. I remember going down the stairs from that upper flat with the zeal of God flooding me, and a desire to stand at every street corner and preach the gospel, absolutely fearlessly, without fear of man or anything in the world. Fear had gone away.

I think most people suffer from fear to some degree or other. You may be afraid of somebody at your work who ridicules you, who can raise a laugh against you. You may be afraid of a bullying employer. You may be afraid of attitudes or influences within your own family. It is absolutely amazing, the number of things which cause fear, and the number of people who live with it constantly. It is a deadly weapon of the devil. Fear of hidden things coming out, fear of the future, fear of circumstances that you are not quite sure about, fear of failure, fear of poverty, fear of ill-health, fear of death for oneself or for friends and loved ones. Fear, fear, fear – bondages of Satan, weapons in the hand of the devil.[7]

Clear out every last stronghold of the devil from your life. Christ came that you might have life, and that you might have it more abundantly. You know what women are like when they spring-clean. They want to get into every corner, into every place that a normal man never thinks about. When Christ comes, He comes to spring-clean:

He will thoroughly cleanse His threshing floor.
(Matthew 3:12)

Let that purging come into every corner of life, into every hidden nook and cranny of it.

In concluding perhaps I should mention that there are many fears that do not just fade away with the passing of time. Often deliverance ministry is needed and we see God move in power again in multiplied lives. The need really is very great. In dealing with fears whether of general or phobic nature, the sufferer is asked to relive a bad experience or otherwise visualize a situation where fear is at its worst. Then he or she is asked to visualize Christ. At the crucial point He is asked to come into the situation and so frequently and so wonderfully He does just that. In masses people are set free.

Notes

[1] The occasion was our July camp, 1993.

[2] Susan Sharkey's story is told in my book *The Incomparable Christ* (New Dawn Books, 1989).

[3] Diana's story is included in *Gospel Vignettes*, part 2.

[4] Whilst a recent commission has come out against such claims, informed sources, such as Dorothy Harper, support them. From my own experience I am left in no doubt.

[5] My daughter Grace Gault is in charge of our Greenock church. Both Diana and Grace speak of the ministry of deliverance in my *Revival: Living in the Realities* (New Dawn Books, 1993), chapter 8.

[6] This chapter deals with fears other than what are regarded as phobias, but from which God would set us free. For further information on the distinction between general fear and particular phobias, see appendix. Details of healings from phobias such as fire, birds and flying are described in my book *Christ the Deliverer* (New Dawn Books, 1991). It should be understood, however, that there are fears which are not bad things necessitating deliverance. They are quite normal and are really there in the will of God for our preservation. For example, it is good that a child should learn to fear fire. This kind of fear is healthy.

[7] Some time ago Alison Speirs preached a sermon which highlighted the prevalence of fear in Christians, particularly fear of people. I was amazed at the numbers who were affected and came for ministry. More recently this was repeated with similar effects. Fear is obviously very deep and very widespread. We ignore this at our peril.

Chapter 3

The Weapons of Christ

Now we turn to consider the arming of the child of God. A strange thing, is the power of the life of God in His people. Consider a mighty state like imperial Rome or the USSR as it was till very recently, with their vast resources, their military potential and their determination to rule the world. In spite of their best efforts, at the end it was obvious they had built on sand. Beneath the surface in both cases there was an ongoing movement of God, whose weapons were not carnal, but spiritual.

> *For our wrestling is not against flesh and blood, but against the principalities, against the powers, against the world-rulers of this darkness, against the spiritual hosts of wickedness in the heavenly places.*
>
> (Ephesians 6:12)

The Christian is clothed with meekness and humility, peace, long-suffering, gentleness, compassion. How are these spiritual weapons ever going to bring down the strongholds of evil? Go back in history to the very earliest Christian times, and you will find that the Man who died on the cross has ruled from the cross, or, perhaps I should say, from the throne. For ever after He has ruled the hearts of men.

By meekness and defeat
  He won the meed and crown,
Trod all His foes beneath His feet
  By being trodden down.

It is the victory of the Lamb, the inoffensive, the meek, the
mild and gentle Jesus.

Let me be more specific.

The Power of Christ

First let me quote the remarks attributed to Napoleon on
the isle of St Helena as I best remember them. He had had
his day of glory, he had made a second attempt at empire,
and there in lonely exile he was pondering the fate of
men and nations and the history of France and Europe,
and he was pondering the Crucified. He said, 'Tonight
there is scarce a sword in Europe that would be un-
sheathed for me, and yet there are millions who would
gladly die for Him. Can this indeed be the Messiah?' To
which we reply, Who else? Who else?

Paul could say,

> *I am not ashamed of the gospel: for it is the power of
> God unto salvation to every one that believeth.*
>
> (Romans 1:16)

Paul standing in the midst of a Roman world, knowing the
power of Rome and the wisdom of Greece, said, *I am not
ashamed of the gospel* – in other words, 'I am proud of the
gospel.' *It is the power of God unto salvation* – and he
might have continued to say: Bring on your Greek philo-
sophers one and all, and show them a dead child. They
may philosophize over it, and they may speak great swel-
ling words of wisdom, but the child remains dead. But
bring in the Lord Jesus: *Damsel, I say unto thee, Arise.*
And she that was dead was restored. The widow of Nain's
son in the open bier, dead and about to be buried: raised

from the dead. The body of Lazarus already in the grave: *Lazarus, come forth!* And he that was bound hand and foot and dead for days came out of that tomb. And as one has said, if Christ had not circumscribed His command by naming him, all the dead of all ages would have come out of all tombs by that word. Yes, Paul could say, *I am proud of the gospel* – 'I am proud of Christ. In the Grecian world I am proud of the wisdom of Christ. And your wisdom pales before the power of Christ.

'And what of you, O Roman? You have broken the nations under your cruel feet, and your Caesars have ascended their thrones over the broken bodies of men. They have sailed through seas of human blood to their desired havens. My Lord gave His own body to be broken, and His own blood to be shed. At your hands he died a cruel death. But see that man in the gutter, that alcoholic, that drug addict, that broken life: what Rome could never do with all its power, Jesus can do. Rome can break the bodies of men, but Christ can remake them. He goes down into the gutters of the world and He raises and He changes and He makes such men and women princes and princesses of God. Yes, you can kill them, but He can make them live again. I am proud of the gospel of Jesus Christ.' And I too am proud of it in this twentieth century. I am proud of Christ, blessed be His name for ever.

God's Weapons

And so we come to the arming of this mild but most powerful army in all the world: the army of the Son of God. An army is made up of individuals, and a church is made up of individuals. You go out not only as a company; you go out as individuals to fight the battle with Satan. And God wants you to have certain weapons.

Faith

He wants you to have **Faith**.

'Oh,' you say, 'we know all about faith. That's easy. We all have faith: without faith it is impossible to please God. We could not come to Christ at all without faith. So you really don't have very much to teach us about faith.'

No? Just hold for a moment.

Another word for faith is trust: quite simply, trust. And you know that in human relationships your trust is built on a foundation of experience. You get to know somebody, but you begin to find that there are flaws in them, and that they do not always keep their word. When the going is rough you can't always depend on them, and basically you have no real faith in them. You know that occasionally they will react aright, but you cannot be sure of it. With other people, the more you get to know them the surer you become that they will never let you down. They are people who keep their word. They are totally loyal. On the basis of experience you trust them. You say, 'If so-and-so said it, they will do it. They will keep their word; they are trustworthy.' Now God expects us to recognize that He is One who can be totally trusted. If He speaks a word of promise to you it will be fulfilled. You need have no doubt or problem about it. It will be absolutely fulfilled, and its fulfilment will not be related to the greatness of the promise. It will be related to the character of God who gives the promise. Always trust Him.

When I am dealing with people for salvation and I come to the matter of assurance I often illustrate this by saying, 'Now, look: Christ has said He receives all who come. Supposing I said to you, "If you come and reach out your hand, I'll give you an expensive fountain pen," and you put out your hand, you would expect to receive the pen because I had given my word. Your faith would depend on your estimate of my character and integrity – not on the value of the thing promised, be it great or small. The basic considerations are these: Am I the kind of person who would tell a lie about it? Do I keep my spoken word? If you judge me to be a man of integrity, you will believe that that pen is as good as yours, because I promised it.

We act that way with each other, and how much more should we trust God?' When God speaks a word, we should depend on it absolutely. Thus when God says,

> *Come unto me, all ye that labour and are heavy laden,*
> (Matthew 11:28 AV)

and you come, you can believe His promise:

> *him that cometh to me I will in no wise cast out.*
> (John 6:37)

Your faith can stand on the character and integrity of the One who makes the promise.

I have never known a word of God fall to the ground. His words never fail. The words of men frequently do, but His words stand for ever. His word is perfect and age-enduring. And He wants you to have faith in Him.

I am not proposing to go in detail down some of the sidelines I have previously written about: the rubbishy things that some people in effect teach, for example, 'Just work yourself into a state of believing, and you'll get whatever you ask,' as though the believing that secures the promise is of human contrivance. This leaves chaos behind it. This is not faith. Faith is a response to the word of God. It does not start in the human heart. The human heart answers, and you trust the word that He gives. **You** don't manufacture the word; **you** don't decide the going. You receive the instruction, and you believe it.

And, you know, faith grows with its exercise. Faith grows with experience. I know this particularly in the operation of gifts. When the ministry of bringing others into the baptism of the Spirit begins, it is wonderful: 'Oh, it happened!' Then the thought comes, 'But it might not always happen!' But when it happens again and again, you get to a stage where you would be absolutely shocked if the normal conditions were being fulfilled and it didn't happen. You just feel that could not be. You enter into a law of receiving, not merely a chance of receiving. And so with other gifts of the Spirit. They deepen with use and experience, until you walk almost beyond faith, almost in the realm of knowledge, it becomes so strong; it grows with the use.

There is another side to it, one that I think must be very hurtful to God, if I can speak of hurt in relation to the divine (and I think one may).

When we say glibly, as if to excuse ourselves, 'Oh, you know, I don't have a lot of faith. My faith is weak,' we sound as though we were making a really humble statement. We speak as though faith were something that can be held, so to speak, in a bottle, and we are unfortunate in not having enough of it. The truth is that we are insulting God. When you say this, you are really saying, 'I judge God to be such a person that you can't trust Him.' When you say, 'I haven't got much faith,' you mean you haven't trust in God. It is offensive language. It is a blasphemy to dare to say that God is not trustworthy. Oh, we have a lot of nice fancy phrases about faith. Analyse them and you will find some of them aren't so fancy. You are insulting the divine by saying you have no faith. I tell you this, that when He speaks and you receive and believe the word and act upon it, you will receive the promise that is given.

I often use this illustration. My oldest daughter Alison was in America for a long time. And I envisage her being at home in conversation with her sister Mary, not knowing I am within earshot. Alison is saying, 'You know, Dad has promised to write to me once a fortnight, but I don't believe him. I don't – I can't trust Dad.' Now if that had happened to you, you might have cast it over your shoulder. I wouldn't. I would carry that to the grave: that a daughter of mine actually didn't trust me. I don't make many promises, but I was taught as a child to keep the promises I did make. And if I had promised Alison that I would write her a lengthy letter once a fortnight, I would have written a lengthy letter once a fortnight. And if I had heard her say, 'I don't trust Dad,' it would have wounded me to the very quick.

Get to know God. If you get to know Him you cannot do anything but trust Him. When He spoke to me on the island of Lewis and showed me the life of Abraham, He spoke as clearly as with an audible voice. I had been through a very tough time, a dark time. It was troubling me; I was introspecting about it. And He said, 'Now in spite of all these things do you believe that I can do this through you?' (indicating the thing He had sent me to Lewis to do). And my spirit said, 'No.' I was shocked on two counts: first, I didn't know a human spirit could speak, and second, I would never have said, 'No,' to God. Very graciously, very tenderly, not harshly or judgmentally, but very quietly, He took me through the life of Abraham and the intended offering of Isaac. At the end of it, He said to me again, 'Now in spite of all these things do you believe that I can do this through you?' This time my spirit said, 'Yes.' It came from the deeps of my being. And I entered the realm of the miraculous: not half an hour later but immediately. I saw miracle after miracle, and have done through all the rest of my life. I have seen thousands come to Christ; I have seen thousands filled with the Holy Spirit; I have seen more people healed and delivered from evil power than I can remember, and much of it from that hour.

He also said something to me very clearly: 'I want you to walk before me as Abraham walked. I do not want you to lean on men or denomination.' There are people who would have loved us to join their denomination, but I have never been free. God spoke to me so clearly: 'Lean on Me, lean on Me; walk with Me, walk with Me.' Now as an older man I can say to you: no word He ever gave me fell to the ground. No work I ever started on my own prospered. Nothing I did worked; nothing He did ever failed. And if I had life to live over again I would believe Him for more than I have done. That is my testimony to the faithfulness of God. And faith is one of the greatest weapons in the kingdom. When He speaks to you and gives you a promise, believe it and act on it.

I want to tell you a little about how we secured some of our first churches and how faith was involved.

When God gave us our first church He gave me a vision on the hillside and I came and looked for where He indicated, not knowing Greenock (I wasn't Greenock born). I stood and I looked at it ... but you can't ask another man for his building. He might not even be saved. For years it remained in my memory until I was asked by a pupil if I was interested in that church, and then by a deacon of it. It was being sold. One after the other they asked me, a year apart. And I had never been really interested in any other church. To cut a long story short, we got that building for £850. And in an odd way others who were interested in it dropped out of the bidding. We got it in time to take thousands of people to the Kelvin Hall in Glasgow, to the Billy Graham meetings.

The money came in the nick of time; it couldn't have come a day earlier; and while the person who was going to loan us a thousand pounds waited in his accountant's anteroom he recognized his brother's footsteps going out of the main office. His brother had been repaying a loan of a thousand pounds that day: the money, or at least the means to secure it, was sitting there on the table.

God spoke to me almost immediately about other three churches locally, and thereafter across the country church after church after church has opened. We have never had any rich people in our congregations, never at any time, with perhaps two exceptions. One rich gentleman came for a month or two and then because of our teaching on divorce, I reckon, he left. We didn't pander, we didn't lower the standard, not for a moment. A second attended for a few months only.

I could tell you of miracle after miracle. And with church after church, He showed clearly what to do; He showed what not to do. He reveals His will, and all you need to do is believe it and act on it. And it's a wonderful adventure. You have not got the money, and you put the plans through as though you had it all! That happened in Larkfield, and in the nick of time the money came. In that case the same gentleman who loaned the money for the purchase of the main Greenock church now offered to sell his investments and loan the church the proceeds. The sum realized was almost to a penny the estimate for the building.

God told me clearly that money for further buildings would not come that way. Day after day I passed vacant ground in Port Glasgow and felt that God had it for a new church. My question was money. He indicated the covenant scheme and I replied that I had already invest-igated that and our accountant had pointed out that it was inappropriate since only a few of us paid standard rate income tax. We were mainly a young congregation then. God said again: 'Covenant scheme.' I bypassed the accountant and went directly to an Inland Revenue inspector who spent about two hours with me explaining in detail how all income tax was recoverable. I put the matter to the church and many responded. I asked God in this case for a sign: if a certain amount came in over one month – significantly more than would normally have been expected – we would go ahead. It did, and we built. In a strange way that I never clearly understood we seemed to have more money in the bank when the build-ing was completed than when we started – with all bills paid. We did much of the work ourselves, labouring for the 'brickies'.

The same pattern was followed in Gourock. Again we did much of the work ourselves and God provided the finance. So church after church was built or acquired. Always God was true to His promise. When you walk with God, I tell you, you find He is a great God. Believe God, and it will be reckoned to you for righteous-ness.

He spoke to me clearly in Lewis these long years ago, and He came and spoke to me again in more recent times about deliverance. It was a wonderful moment. It was as though He said, 'Will you take another commission?' I was sitting in a car outside a hospital in Glasgow. He said, 'The first commission in Pentecost didn't make you popular. You carried a cross.' And I had never noticed, because I carried it with great pride: I loved Pentecost; it was a glorious banner. I fought to the gates of hell for Pentecost. There came deep family division. I realized as I looked back – yes, I did carry a cross; but I had not particularly noticed it as such. While I had felt the pain of family discord I never thought of it in terms of my carrying a cross. I was intensely proud of Pentecost.

He said, 'Will you take another commission?' I said, 'Yes.' He said, 'Neither will this make you popular.' Had it not been God I would have quipped, 'So what's new?' But when God speaks I am reverent, and I said no word. He let me know I was to carry a message of deliverance and cleansing to the church prior to the coming of Christ. Friends, do you know that from that hour, for years there was scarcely a week passed that people were not delivered, sometimes from demons of long standing. He was true to His word, blessed be the name of the Lord.

You must move in faith, which is just trust in the heavenly Father. You can do nothing of yourself; it has got to come from God.

At the present time, with the erection of a building costing about half-a-million pounds, He has called for faith.[1] But never think in terms of big faith, little faith, strong faith, weak faith. Think of the One in whom the faith is placed. Ask the one essential question: is God in the matter? Is our course of action the will of God? If so, it does not matter whether the cost will be half-a-million, or double. It is essential to hear His word and follow it scrupulously. **If a project is in the will of God and we are obedient, it will come into being.** That is one of the fundamental principles I am teaching.[2]

Prayer

The second weapon that has come to mind is the weapon of **Prayer**. If we had endless time, I'd say, 'Jessie, would you come up here and tell the company about the Monday morning prayer meeting which you lead?'[3] I have been greatly impressed with Jessie's introduction to these prayer sessions. You can feel the throb of God, the drive of God, the assurance that God is in this matter and that He will hear and answer our prayers. An hour passes remarkably quickly, because it is a God-called prayer meeting, and God is moving in it.

In speaking of prayer I have to be very careful, especially in critical remarks, because I believe that God knows every aspiration of His every child. A new-born babe in Christ, indeed a person not even saved but in honesty and sincerity seeking God, is heard. I believe God hears every word. But I also believe there are some of our prayers that in another sense He doesn't hear. When we have come to Christ and have fallen into bad habits, with our prayers becoming almost a commandment of men, and we think we will be heard for our much asking, and are not God-centred but self-centred, I imagine many of these prayers don't get past the ceiling.

What is prayer? It should be a response to God. You come into His presence, you wait for His word and for the impression He puts on your spirit. You respond to this in simplicity. It can be in very quiet language, both in the home and in the church. Never associate volume with power. It can of course be loud; there is no blueprint about this. There are times when prayer should be very definite and clear-cut and loud. There are other times when it should be very quiet and gentle. Again let me say: the power is not necessarily related to the volume of the utterance. Prayer should be real and it should be sincere. Basically it should be under the unction of the Spirit. And I would say to those of you baptized in the Holy Spirit that you should never pray publicly at any time other than under the unction of the Spirit. Neither should you preach other than under the unction of the Spirit. Indeed, you should never live other than under the power of the Spirit. It is not a case of, 'Oh, I've got to come under unction before I pray!' You should have an anointing that abides. You should come into church gatherings ready to pray.

Many years ago God impressed on me that I should live in such a way that at any moment I could leave whatever I was doing and pray for a person's baptism in the Spirit, for example, without having to get anything in my life sorted or brushed out of the road. I had to live that way. And if you live that way you can pray under unction, you can speak under unction. In your conversations with people, in all the ways of life, you should be looking for the touch of the Spirit, the unction of the Spirit. God wants us to come up higher into a spiritual dimension where we operate as spiritual creatures, leaving the earth life far below and forever being in touch with the living God. Is that too much for you? That is the New Testament pattern. I do not know any other way; there is no other way. We are to live in the light of eternity. We are to live that way.

This particularly touches prayer. You will find that there are people who have a special gift in prayer, a special ministry and a special call. There are people who become intercessors. They are like Moses, who interceded for Israel and saved a nation. They are like Praying Hyde who moved mightily for God in India, and Farmer Nash who worked with Finney in America. You find across the pages of history men who came under mighty anointings of God in prayer. In that inner realm they took strongholds, they gripped the kingdom and they took men and women captive for Christ. They changed situations, they changed communities, they changed nations. One of the most important ministries in all the world is that deep ministry of prayer. I remember one who came and told me that opportunity had been given in the inner world to be a prayer warrior. She looked at the place, but it seemed very obscure and unattractive, and she turned it down. Yes, she turned it down. Yet this is one of the most important places in all the world: the place of deep prayer.

I believe that prayer will increase amongst us as we come nearer the end. I thank God for more in our own companies who are having the burden of prayer, intercessory prayer. Absolutely vital and fundamental is prayer.

There is another aspect of prayer. You may have been shocked by my earlier statement to the effect that 'if you are in trouble, never pray about it.' The meaning was quite simple: if you pray about your trouble, you will concentrate on it, and it is likely to get worse and worse. Let God touch your trouble, and praise Him for the victory. Now you will maybe get an equal shock from something else I am going to say. I think some of the deepest praying that is ever done is totally silent: not one word uttered. Under the power of the Spirit, sharing the agony of the Son of God, the spirit can pray. There may be inner groaning or exclamations of pain as you bear the burden. You obtain the victory in the inner chamber, and you don't talk. We are greatly addicted to talk. In that deepest place we may at times not talk at all. Furthermore, in the time you spend before God, let nine-tenths of it be in listening. Some people can scarcely hear the other side of a conversation without interrupting.

There was a very amusing conversation in one branch of our family which shall be nameless. The mother of the family is a monumental interrupter. On this occasion her daughter was speaking, and the mother suddenly said, 'Excuse **me**,' to which the daughter replied, 'You think that by saying, "Excuse me," you have an immediate right to interrupt!' It had become a habit, and the daughter was having none of it. When God is speaking, don't say a word. Listen and remember. Let what He says be imprinted on your inner consciousness. Three words may be allowed: 'Thank you, Lord.' Maybe that is all He will expect from you. Or just simply, 'Yes, Lord. Yes, Lord.'

Get into a realm which in many ways is above mere human words. We tend to be 'word' people: talk, talk, talk. As though when we talk about something we solve the problem! Quite often we deepen the problem by over-talking. Of course there are times when we should talk – times when we pour out our hearts in vocal prayer. But get the balance right. Learn to listen. Learn the realm of voiceless, wondrous prayer.

The Word of God

So He is putting the faith weapon and the prayer weapon in your hand. He also wants to give you the weapon of the **Word of God**. Learn the word of God. Read it faithfully, regularly and deeply. Become familiar with it. Learn key passages by heart. Immerse yourself in the word. And when the devil comes to you, as he came to Christ, use it as He did. Watch the reaction of Christ to temptation. Again and again He used the word in resisting the devil. In the wilderness Satan came to Him, and on the points of temptation Christ answered him with the word of God. The word is sharper than a two-edged sword (Hebrews 4:12), and it is effective for the pulling-down of strongholds. Be much in the word, know it, use it, and listen as the word speaks to you.

These three: faith, prayer and the word of God, are weapons. There are also conditions with which weapons are associated.

Obedience

If you can become an **obedient** person, totally submissive to God, your life will be blessed, and there will be a weapon in the hand of God that will be effective to the pulling down of the strongholds of hell.

An example I frequently cite is that of a man greatly used of God, a shy, kindly, good man. People wanted to know the secret of his success. He was very reluctant to speak. But ultimately he said (and I paraphrase the story as best I recollect it), 'There was a time when I used to obey God as it suited my convenience. Sometimes I obeyed, sometimes I postponed obedience, and sometimes I didn't really obey at all. But there came a day when it occurred to me that if the great God of Heaven deigned to whisper to me, I should obey immediately. From that day on I have done so, and constant blessing has flowed in my life.'

It won't always be convenient to respond, I may say. You will have something else to do – but when you learn that God takes priority, that His word, His command, takes priority, and you obey, blessing will flow in your life.

I find it difficult to overestimate the importance of obedience. I can sense something here. I know that if I am working for God, and I have those of you with me who are working under my authority, I cannot stand disobedience. I cannot stand a shadow of it, a suspicion of it. I cannot allow a person to exercise their own human mind if they are acting under my spiritual authority. Now I don't mean that in a harsh sense, but there is inside me a total demand for obedience to the God under whose authority I am myself operating. And if I feel like that, what does God feel? What does He feel? Puny worm sits up on its tail and says, 'No, I'm not going to do it this way.' That is what you are like when you disobey God. You have nothing to do but obey Him. But, you say, 'I don't understand.' You don't need to understand – who said you had any right to understand? All you need to know is the instruction: nothing else. All you need to know is what you are to do, and when. He is under no obligation to give an explanation of His ways or an account of Himself to any, none at all. What He does and why He does it is His business. Much of our trouble comes from failing to recognize this, and our failure to recognize it stems from our bad upbringing as children.

The realm of obedience in relation to children is a subject in which my own thinking has undergone a change. I remember disagreeing profoundly with Miss Taylor many years ago. She said, 'When you are training a child, you should not feel obliged to explain. When you give an instruction to do something, do not explain why.'

I thought, 'That is ridiculous. You should let the child know why it should do such-and-such.'

'No,' she said, 'don't do it that way. Teach the child obedience, and when the child obeys it may be in order to give an explanation then. But never make understanding the basis of obedience.'

In training a dog you train it to sit, for example. It may be in the middle of a room and just on its way to a bone. It sees no reason for sitting, but it has got to learn to do this when told – not because it understands it, but because it is told. Obedience is taught. Now the reason for this is that one day it may be leaving a pavement and about to go under an unseen car. Its master sees what it does not see, and calls, 'Sit!' It flops down on the pavement and saves its life.

Miss Taylor taught that it was that kind of obedience that should be instilled into children by their parents. She maintained that initially parents should stand in the place of God, so that when the child learned full obedience it would be easy for it to transfer this attitude to God when it emerged into the spiritual dimension. In short, children should do what they are told because they are told, not because they understand why they are told. I did not initially agree with this teaching, feeling it was going a bit too far. But I came to see things differently. Let me explain. If you are a child of independent mind, and you get a lot of your own way, you are apt to argue if you are thwarted. I was guilty of this myself as a boy. My dad died when I was very young and I argued with my mother a great deal. Do you know that when you come into the spiritual world, deep down you retain the same attitude: 'If I argue about it I'll maybe get my own way. If I cry enough I may be accommodated.' I see this again and again as young people emerge into the spiritual world: they often take issue with God, because they have taken issue with their parents and got away with it. We all have to learn to do what God says, with blind faith. In His great grace He often shows later on why He has given certain instructions. But never make understanding the basis of obedience. We should be living such lives that we are in the place of God, in one sense, to our children. When we are thoroughly obedient servants, we are in a position to react to His slightest whisper. And He has in His hand a powerful and an effective weapon in such obedience.

Endurance

The next weapon on my list is **Endurance**, or stickability. You may have reacted earlier to my comments on self-pity, and many should be reacting right now because the quality of real endurance is comparatively rare.

'I am going right ahead on God's road,' you said, but you met a giant and you turned aside, or you fell over a boulder and sat there nursing your knee.

'Oh, I don't feel like it today. Last week I was in really good form; I was going right on for God. But, you see, this has happened, and that has happened, and the other has happened, and I am lying at the side of the road letting life wash over me, and the devil is wiping his feet on me – and I want to go back into a place of shelter where I don't feel all this . . . ' Endurance? Stickability?

What does it matter how you are feeling? God didn't ask you anything about your feelings. He asked you to do what you were told. He pointed you on a road; all you have to do is walk that road, and if you are tripped up you get up and go on; if you are persecuted you go on. Paul could say, 'I press on.' They lashed him and they tried to kill him, the devil tried to drown him, he was in peril of a hundred kinds, and he said, 'I press on to the prize of the high calling of God.'

You say, 'You are pushing it. You are extreme.'

Nothing of the kind; I am only paddling in the shallow

water as yet. I tell you, they left that man's body lying outside the gates of Lystra, having stoned him, thinking he was dead. And he got up and walked away. He didn't go down to the coast for a time of refreshing, either, or for six months' holiday. Nor did he retire from the battle because he had suffered so deeply. He didn't say, 'A whole lot of other Christians haven't suffered as much as I have, and why should I go on suffering?' He had one driving purpose: to bring the knowledge of God into that ancient world. **I press on**: disregarding all the physical suffering, all the mental persecution from the Judaizers, he went on.

You make your decision, and I often like this kind of decision made in cold blood without undue emotion because an able preacher in a wonderful emotional meeting can get people to do remarkable things. If you had one of these preachers promising that prosperity would follow you for evermore, you might be prepared to do many things and really loosen your purse strings. I have heard of one preacher raising money at a time when a hundred pounds was a very large sum: 'Who will give a hundred pounds? Who will give fifty pounds?' Down to five pounds, one pound. And then he evidently held up ball-point pens. 'Now these ball-point pens have been blessed. Who'll give thirty pence for a blessed ball-point pen?' I would have left all the blessed ball-point pens with him. You may find an able preacher who will manipulate a congregation badly, and woe betide him!

I remember one famous preacher's finance manager trying to manipulate a meeting where I was present. It was in my earlier days, when half-a-crown meant something. I was on the platform because I was a leader, sitting like a stookie[4] with a lot of other leaders, when the finance manager came on. He started by reviling the congregation because on the previous night there had been some people who hadn't put notes in the offering; they had merely put in silver! Shame upon them! Tonight it should be the biggest note people had in their pockets! As it happened, one of our folks had an unsaved friend with her, present in such a meeting for the first time. This lady fished in her pocket for the biggest note she had, until her Christian friend prevented her from parting with it. A first touch in an evangelical meeting: the biggest note she had! And I was sitting there with this precious half-crown. But not for long – because I changed it for one of these old baffle-wall threepenny-bits. The only reason I put it in was to save my face when the basket came round, and I wasn't so tough then as I am now; I hope I would have the courage not to put in any now. That's true.

Oh, yes, people can be manipulated. I don't want merely to stir an emotional atmosphere and have you say, 'Yes, I'll go all the way with God. I feel good tonight, I really feel the blessing on my soul tonight.' I want you to **be** good and to **do** good when you don't feel the blessing on your soul. I want you to act as I was prepared to do when I didn't know Christ, and was desperate to find Him and could not. I was prepared to sit at the gates of heaven for a lifetime, even if He never took me. I was prepared to live the Christian life to the best of my ability. I actually did that, friends. These are not just words. I did that. And within an hour or thereabouts I was born of the Spirit: I was born again. I had made a cool decision to go right on forever. And there is no reason why any one of you should not make that absolute choice to go all the way with God. Let the cry be, 'As for me and my house we will serve the Lord without qualification, modification, or condition.' An absolute and a complete surrender.

There was a young Christian who thought I was tough with him when he came for ministry in Wales and was chased away twice until he was desperate. I am similarly tough with people who come to negotiate terms of salvation. I say, 'Look, I have nothing for you until you are prepared to surrender absolutely, unconditionally, for time and eternity. If you are not prepared to do that, I haven't another word to say to you.' Absolute surrender is the demand of the living God. When that condition is met, endurance is not difficult afterwards. You are not led to expect that you will be made comfortable. You don't take any thought for whether you will feel good. You are far more concerned with duty than with rights. The word **ought** comes into your vocabulary: 'What ought I to do?' not 'What do I feel like doing?'

'What ought I to do?' Is there a meeting for which you are carrying a responsibility, but it doesn't really suit you to be consistent? You would rather do this or that. Take a recent camp situation, for example. There were people in need, to whom others were ministering, and there could have been counter attractions with the weather becoming warm. It was not a matter of what people felt like doing, but a matter of what they ought to do. They went on ministering, and it affected their afternoon. Get the word **ought** back into your vocabulary. And get the word **endurance** into your heart as an essential way of life. Christ Himself endured. We too can endure as seeing Him who is invisible. Despise the shame, grasp the cross. And if you feel a little ill-done-to and find a little self-pity rising, go and read of the sufferings of Christians behind the Bamboo Curtain and the Iron Curtain of earlier days. Read a bit about what Richard Wurmbrand and others came through, and you will maybe learn something about endurance.

To any of you who are lacking in endurance, I recommend *Bruchko* (formerly titled *For This Cross I'll Kill You*).[5] It portrays the endurance of a man almost beyond believing. The glory of God has been on that life.

I wonder how many of you are attracted to endurance? I wonder how many of you are prepared to say, 'Yes, Lord, give me endurance, no matter what it costs. Lord, that is a weapon that I could do with. I'd like to get my hand on that sword.' Endurance, stickability, the quality of keeping at it.

A training in farming would do many people a world of good. An old uncle of mine had a very memorable saying when he and I were working together. We were moving a big pile of stones. It was a very big pile when we started, and it was a big pile for quite a time thereafter. We were using an old wheelbarrow to take the stones elsewhere. 'Och aye,' he would say, 'you just caw awa', you caw awa'.' I had never heard **caw awa'** before – you just 'keep at it'. You kept at it, and after a time the pile had disappeared.

I am currently working on a manuscript which will interest many of you. It centres around the teachings of Miss Taylor, revealing some of the mystic, inner aspects of spiritual life.[6] Some of the revelation is wonderful and will be very helpful, and some will convey stern warning. There are items in her confict with hell that could alarm some. In the watches of the night I have been working on the notes, and it can be a slow business. I transcribe maybe half-a-dozen or eight pages of the notebook at a time, and I recall the expression, 'You just caw awa'.' The bit you don't do tonight will be there for you tomorrow. You just keep at it and do it bit by bit. And it is amazing how you get through it. You plod on. In the Christian walk, there is a great deal of plodding. Don't make any mistake about that. All Christian life does not consist of glory meetings. It also involves grey Monday morning meetings with the unsanctified. You are dealing with life in the raw, right down on earth. But you keep going for God wherever you are, in all circumstances.

I feel that some of this teaching is getting through. I feel in my bones that a lot of the shoes that I am handing out are fitting very well, and maybe some of them are even pinching toes because you haven't been as powerfully regular and devoted and strong as you should have been. We can never think of Christ deviating. Did you ever realize that the devil is always active? There are no holidays with him. Through our annual holiday period, souls are still pouring into hell. The devil never sleeps, nor does Christ. Their work goes on. And Christ is utterly dependable, He is utterly stable, and He will transmit these qualities to you if you will. If you have no backbone when you come to Christ, He'll give you one. He'll kill the jellyfish in you, and He'll give you a spine. He'll make a man or a woman of you, with stability in the heart of you.

I recommend the sentiments of the following poem for your consideration:[7]

> More than half beaten, but fearless,
>   Facing the storm and the night,
> Reeling and breathless, but fearless,
>   Here in the lull of the fight.
> I who bow not but before Thee,
>   God of the fighting clan,
> Lifting my fists I implore Thee,
>   Give me the heart of a man!
>
> What though I stand with the winners,
>   Or perish with those that fall?
> Only the cowards are sinners;
>   Fighting the fight, that is all.
> Strong is my foe, who advances,
>   Snapped is my blade, O Lord;
> See their proud banners and lances,
>   But spare me the stub of a sword!

Courage

The next weapon I have noted is **Courage**.

Studd used to speak of heroism as the lost chord of Christianity. That All England cricketer (and couldn't England do with him now![8]) gave up his cricket, gave up his career, went as a missionary to China and to India, was invalided home and found no committee to support him. Becoming a museum of diseases, he took as his committee God the Father, Son and Holy Spirit, and under the banner 'If Jesus Christ be God and died for me, then no sacrifice can be too great that I can make for Him,' he sailed to evangelize a world. He saw the vast, teeming millions of Africa, the part to which he was at that time particularly called (although God called him ultimately to the whole unevangelized world). He had his mission to the tribes of Africa, to people living in fearful conditions, oppressed by hell. He saw this not as a chore but as a glorious challenge and opportunity. There was still something to be done on earth in the service of the Son of God. Christ was calling for brave men and women who would sacrifice their all for Him and for the gospel. Studd gathered around him a band of like-minded people, but to his sorrow some who were not like-minded split off. He was a man of strong, indomitable character. His attitude was: 'Go forward for God.'

Should a young missionary ask, 'What will I get for food?' Studd is reputed to have said, 'Gather the berries from the trees, you'll get food as you go.'

'And what if we don't get food?'

'Then you'll die, and you'll be promoted to glory from the front line.' What greater honour could you ever have than being a martyr for the cause of God?

'But death's a terrible tragedy.'

'Not at all. Death is a translation into the eternal glory for a child of God,' we could imagine him saying. He was determined that under God he would drive the gospel into the heart of Africa, and he drove the gospel into the heart of Africa. In the afterward he found that thousands of the converts 'had a name that they lived', but in his opinion they were dead so far as deep holiness was concerned. He split the movement right down the centre. Without holiness no man shall see God (Hebrews 12:14). The faction who opposed him said, 'You are teaching salvation by works,' to which he replied, 'I am doing no such thing. If you have faith, I'll see the works, and if I don't see a Holy Ghost church in Africa, men and women full of God and of holiness, my work has failed.' He set a standard and he kept a standard. He didn't just go around preaching mere words. He went out into the forefront of the battle and he showed by his own life the qualities of heroism and courage. Oh yes, he was a man of character.

Do you recall his jingles?

> Round and round the nursery floor
> Let us perambulate:
> Sugar and spice and all things nice
> Must be on our plate.

And what about the call to the mission field and the lack of men? I cannot remember all he wrote, but one famous piece intoned, 'Lord, don't send me; send my sister.' There are far more women on the field than men: about six to one. The lost chord of heroism, of courage – can you not feel it stirring in your soul? Would you not like to mount a white war-horse and get into the battle and, if you die, let all your wounds be in front? Oh, that I might stir you to courage and endurance!

Studd reckoned that the world needed to see a generation of heroic people who would go to all lengths for Jesus Christ. Where is the red badge of courage, of heroism? Again I recommend the book *Bruchko*, already referred to, where you will see something of modern courage, modern heroism, modern sacrifice, a life sold out for God. And if you do not feel ashamed, then you are a better man than I am.

I thank God for the courage some of you do show. I was impressed with how many of you came out on to Sauchiehall Street[9] recently. In other words, you said, 'Let my neighbours and my friends see me preaching here if they will. I don't care whether they do or not.'

It is not everybody who thinks you are socially acceptable if you are preaching, with or without a soapbox, on the open street. Quite a number of us have nice friends, very respectable friends. I used to move in high educational circles! Indeed, I once found myself invited to Holyrood Palace. There I sat with nobility. I remember one of them chatting about her friend Willie – who was Willie Whitelaw. And, well, that was OK by me. It was just an accident that the Queen herself wasn't present (this was at the time of the opening of a general assembly of the Church of Scotland in Edinburgh). I suppose I had been invited to Holyrood because I was the chairman of a national educational committee.

True to form, by the time of my arrival I had a puncture. You know what it's like to change a puncture, and go in and shake hands with the Queen's Commissioner. I was in quite a dilemma. I got to the Palace before the tyre was too flat, but I knew I was in real difficulty. It would be absolutely flat by the time I came back out. I explained my problem to the equerry. 'Sir,' he said, 'don't trouble about it at all! Just give me the keys of your boot, and we'll fix it for you.' Now if you had seen the state of my boot . . . ! It was unspeakable. But anyway, I was never likely to meet the equerry again, so – 'There are the keys.' And I went away in and dined royally!

I carried on open-air meetings for years, and when I was in jail one night for doing so Mr Robert Cleary[10] kept the meeting going. (I have only recently learned that when he went eventually to the jail on that night so long ago to find how I was and when I would be released, he was given thirty seconds to get out or he would be put in beside me!) We had great times in open-air days. It really was very exciting, very wonderful at times. God saved souls; scores of people professed salvation in open-air days. Hundreds gathered before we even got there. The crowds were there, God was there, and souls were saved.

Then I became a teacher. Oh, dear. I was told later that some of the staff in my first school were waiting for my arrival. I had preached at open-air meetings! I had been in court twice! In court for holding open-air meetings – and now a teacher! It was not at all proper! You could feel it, and it does not do you any harm to feel some things. It helps to give you a backbone. The tables turned all round about before the day was done. Yes, the memories flood back. I do appreciate that there are many of you in this generation who are prepared to stand up and be counted in public. Thank God for it.

Communion

The next one is a strange one. It is a condition, and if you
find the condition, God has a tremendous weapon. It is
Communion. Now immediately people think of the taking
of the emblems. There is such a lot of writing about the
taking of the bread and the wine, and such an ignorance
of what communion really means in the sense in which I
am using it. It means a relationship with Christ, a being
close to the Lord Jesus, so that His life emanates through
you. Mary[11] was speaking of spiritual bonds that are
forged by Christ, and the strength that comes with these
bonds. When a company comes into revival power,
the bonds grow wondrous strong. The basic bond is the
bond with Christ Himself. The soul goes into a place of
union and communion with God.

This is central to all life. The door is closed, and the soul
is centred on Christ, not on work for Christ, not on other
people, not in any relationship in all the world, but bound
to Christ. Work should not be central but should flow out
from that relationship. 'Give me first a little meal: give me
first a little oil.[12] Give Me first the love of your heart.'
Let there be a love relationship between the soul and
Christ, and life will flow out from that glorious relationship. Never default on this; never put it into a low
category. Never be so busy even with the work of God
that this is neglected. Make love for Christ the first
priority.

The soul who finds this place goes out into the world,
and that relationship with Christ holds firm. The life of
Christ comes emanating through such people. They go
into a company and the atmosphere changes. They begin
to speak and the atmosphere changes. The touch of Christ
is there. It can reveal itself in the accent, in the tone of the
voice, in the lovelight in the eyes. It can be in the gentleness of movement. It can be in the way in which a man or
a woman walks. Your walk can show arrogance and pride,
or it can show humility and grace. You must have the

whole being suffused by God. That can happen, and I tell you, when you meet someone to whom it has happened, it is truly wonderful. You feel the sense of the fragrance of Christ.

There is a lovely description of a valley in Roumania which is filled with roses.[13] At certain times of the year people need only to be in there for a very short time, and they will smell of roses for the rest of the day. The scent permeates their garments and goes with them. If you go into the garden of God, where Christ is, you will find a fragrance that will touch your garments, and wherever you go His fragrance will go with you: the fragrance of Christ. Let your communion be deep with Christ, and it will affect lives. Some you will speak to, and they will feel it. Some will pick it up without speech. Of all the weapons I have taken, this is perhaps the most essential: communion with Christ. We tend to be more taken up with working for God than in loving God, in doing something for our fellow men than in spending time in conscious union with God. Now union with God is fundamental. Working for God is secondary, and work flows out of union. Pay attention to union and communion.

Love

Similarly fundamental in the Christian's weaponry is **Love**.

God taught me a lesson in three stages where love is concerned. (This story has been told in earlier writing, but to give this book the required balance I outline it again.) In the first stage, a man dealt very bitterly and cruelly with me. I was in a position to fix him, and I was intending to fix him, as the Americans would say, real good. As I was pondering my revenge and enjoying the prospect, God spoke to me and said, 'I love that man.' I wanted to hear nothing about it. I walked on a few steps, and Christ said, 'Do you think you are better than I, that you can afford to hate where I forgive?' or words to that effect. That stopped me in my tracks, and God showed me in a moment of time that He didn't want me to love what that man was; He wanted me to love what that man could be in Christ: love him into a different and a better position. I understood it; the burden rolled away, and I took no revenge.

The years passed, I was baptized in the Spirit, and there was fearful family resentment. Two of my brothers shot my dog. Now that would have been enough for almost a murder at an earlier stage, because I have always been very fond of dogs. I was particularly fond of that dog. And that dog got shot, really, as a result of following me because of his love for me. I was very bitter, but God spoke to me. My life was at a critical stage, and I had a choice to make: to go for God or to take revenge. I died to revenge and I went for God, and my life took a spiritual leap that day.

You might say, 'Well, you were home and dry then.' I thought I was home and dry, but circumstances came round where I was being bitterly persecuted by one of the two, and I was feeling it sore. I got to the point where I was prepared to forgive him because I knew as a Christian I had to forgive. Then it was as though God said to me, 'I am not interested in your forgiving him. I want you to love him.' That was too much for me! 'I want you to love him.' Oh, that was bitter medicine. I was not willing, but I suppose I was willing to be made willing. I went down on my knees by my bedside alone, and opened my heart to the love of Christ. I knew that He had stood far worse pain for me than I was being asked to stand for Him – and His love swept in. My life was transformed in a moment of time. I literally mean transformed. I suddenly found that that man's power to hurt was broken, and I had obtained a victory of a kind that 'overcometh the world'; my enemy had no more power over me ever after. His power was broken by the power of love. It is one of the most effective and strongest weapons in the whole universe, the power of love. Not forgiveness, but love, driving love – the love that drove from the cross to the redemption of the worst men in the world, the Jerusalem sinners. 'Tarry at Jerusalem. Preach the gospel, beginning at Jerusalem.' To the crucifiers of Christ the love of God went out. To the very worst of men that love went out. The weapon of love is exceedingly potent.

Humility

Have you ever noticed the power of **Humility**? Have you ever noticed the attractiveness of humility? Now I don't mean the Uriah Heep kind of 'See 'ow 'umble a man I am.' It is the real, deep humility, where people have no exaggerated opinion of themselves at all. They think of others, they put others forward, they are self-effacing. The grace of God is on their lips and in their actions. I find humility an exceedingly attractive quality and have always been quick to recognize and admire it in others.

I have met it, albeit very seldom. I met it in one man whom I only saw for a short time, but the effect of it has remained with me for a lifetime. He was so self-effacing, kind and Christ-like. May I speak of Hudson Taylor again? One lady who knew of his work and greatly desired to know him better had the privilege of entertaining him for a week, and at first she was desperately disappointed. He did not come into her home with the attitude, 'I'm God's man for the hour.' He did not silently proclaim, 'Feel the firmness of my handshake, feel my strength: I am a prince of God. Don't you know who I am?' He came in very quietly and sat down and played with the children. She was so disappointed . . .

Within about two days she was wondering if it was an angel of God she was entertaining: Christ so deeply emanated through him.

Another who comes to mind is Billy Graham. You might think there would be a bit of pride there – that man has been mightily used of God. I watched him carefully on the one occasion when I was on a platform beside him in the Kelvin Hall, Glasgow, in the fifties. You can tell a great deal if you are close enough to a person. Humility or pride is reflected in the way they move their hands and in the tone of their voice and the way they walk to the platform when they rise to preach. Through all the years I never saw a trace of pride in Billy Graham – and I think that the absence of pride is one reason God has used him so deeply. In this humble man of God we see the attraction and the power of humility!

Compassion

There is a whole further list of Christlike characteristics which become weapons in the hand of a servant of God. I am not going in great detail into them. There is **meekness**, which is a bedfellow of humility. There is **Compassion**, which is an aspect of love. A wonderful word, compassion, often associated with Christ: He had *compassion on the multitude* (Mark 8:2). In thinking of a particular life in which there are tremendous disadvantages and a great amount of need, I suddenly felt compassion: just simple, sheer compassion. God loves that poor soul; God loves that broken life. You might say, 'Well, they brought a lot of that on themselves, and they've lived this way and they've lived that way...' Forget it. Christ loves them.

> Just as I am, without one plea,
> But that Thy blood was shed for me
> And that Thou bid'st me come to Thee,
> O Lamb of God, I come.

There is no law against love, there is no law against compassion. Where there are love and compassion, you don't need law. These fulfil the law of Christ spontaneously.

Compassion is a wonderful word. It has a different flavour from love. It is full of love, but it has an element of pity in it. An incident that illustrates this comes from the time when I was a headmaster and drugs made their appearance in this locality. I came head-on against the abuse and was being very bitterly persecuted by certain sections of the Press. At a critical moment, about midnight one night, I was really being pursued by dark forces. I picked up a book of Amy Carmichael's, and it envisaged exactly the position I was in. Quoting Proverbs 31:8 (*'Open thy mouth for the dumb in the cause of all such as are appointed to destruction'* AV), she spoke of the pillory that awaited the one who uncovered 'some hidden sore of his day and generation'.[14] It was an almost perfect picture of what I was feeling. And I had one of these rare experiences of going out of the body – not totally, but partially. I saw the cross of Christ, and I saw Christ on the cross; I'll never forget it. He was facing outwards, towards where I was. There was a great ditch lying between, and the off-scourings of humanity were in that ditch. They were in a terrible state, the drug addicts, the drunkards, the refuse of earth. Meantime the demons were tearing at the body of Christ with steel-like talons: they were ripping His very flesh. And as He looked out, it was as though He totally ignored them, and His love came pouring out, and He let me know that it was for the very worst of men. I felt the compassion of Christ as I had never felt it in all my life: not love for me, but the compassion of Christ for others, and something of it entered into me, and from that day to this I have never despised any son or daughter of Adam's race (not that I was ever prone to do so). The love of Christ is past my telling or communicating easily to you.

He asked me if I would share His cross and go the whole way in the matter in which I was involved. I said, 'Yes, I will.' I shared that cross. And I know something of the compassion of Christ ... the compassion.

And a Fountain of Qualities

Other weapons include self-effacement (keeping out of the

picture, thinking each of others as better than oneself)
peace, joy, long-suffering, righteousness, goodness – again
things against which there is no law. They are all attributes of the Lord Jesus. Basically, put on the Lord Jesus
Christ, and He will send you out into the battle not only
with a number of weapons, but also with the ability to use
them. And once He has these things in place watch Him
do with us as He did with Joshua. Do you remember what
happened to Joshua? Suddenly someone appeared on the
scene, and Joshua went up to him and said, *'Are you come
for us or against us?' 'I am come as the commander of the
Lord's host'* (see Joshua 5:13–14). In other words, 'Joshua,
get out of the road. Joshua, step aside. You thought you
were going to lead the armies of God: I, a spiritual being,
am going to lead the armies of God, and you will do what
you are told, Joshua. If you are told to blow the trumpet
and march round the city, you will do that. If on the
seventh day you are told to go round it seven times and do
such-and-such, you will do just that. You will have no
ideas of your own, Joshua; you will do what I tell you, for
I am the commander of the Lord's hosts.' And Jericho
came tumbling down. Joshua acting on his own could
have blown trumpets for the rest of a lifetime, and Jericho
would metaphorically have stood there laughing at him.
But not when the commander of the Lord's hosts was in
the field.

Look at all the weapons and say, 'Yes, Lord, that one,
that one. Lord, thanks. I want them all.' And at the end of
the day watch for Jesus coming and saying, 'Now, I want
to live in you. Would you kindly empty out all of **you** and
be filled with **Me**, and I will use the weapons, I will secure
the victory, and I will bring revival. You will be an instru-
ment in My hand, and you will show stickability, and
courage, and endurance. You will know the reality of
faith and of prayer, and you will use the word of God. I
will be in you to work through you, and I will show My
love and My compassion and My grace. And I, if I be
lifted up, will draw all men.' It is Christ that people want

to see: Jesus moving through human lives. And, you know, the devil hasn't a chance. I'd hate to be in the devil's army; I'd hate to be trying to operate with his weapons. I tell you this: don't you use his weapons either. Never use his weapons: vengeance and spite and hatred and all the rest of them. Don't touch his tools. They will soil you and weaken you.

Standing back from the battlefield, I see in my spirit that no matter how badly the battle seems to be going in any particular instance, all I need to behold is the white horse of Christ and Christ mounting and entering the lists. Every battle He ever enters may be turned by the power of God. We have a commander who in His own right and strength alone could crush all the power of the enemy. It is good to fight a good fight, and it is wonderful to be fighting on the side of the angels.

Have you ever been in a fight and got the worst of it? I managed to pick fights as a boy. I picked them with older boys and got my nose punched and bleeding and sore, and eyes blackened. I remember lying in bed one morning and trying to hide from my mother the fact that I had two black eyes. The colour had developed handsomely over-night into a mixture of green and yellow and black. I tried, unsuccessfully, to camouflage this with flour. Then when I got up I almost cut the tip of one finger off with a saw-knife. I had to get that plastered, and for the first time in my life I nearly fainted. I should not have gone to school, but I had to go to school – I would not have anybody say that I got such a hammering the day before that I couldn't come to school. Over my dead body! I had a fair share of pride, I can tell you. I was even proud of my pride. And I went to school.

But how good it is to be on the winning side. It is good to know that you have the angels with you and that Christ has entered the battlefield. Wonderful is our privilege, to be born near the end of time, when Christ Himself will appear in glory. I remember Katherine Kuhlman saying there had been a stage in her life when she had wanted

Christ to take her home, the suffering was so intense, but she said in effect, 'Not now. I see now the action of God, the moving of the power of God, and I want my whole life-work to be accomplished before I go into that eternal Presence.' You know, I feel exactly the same. I don't want to go before I render up a full account. I would love to see at least the beginnings of revival before I go. Blessed be His name.

> *Prayer*: Lord, we appreciate that the subject is so vast and so lovely and wonderful, it is very difficult to draw it to a close; there is so much meat that lies here. We pray that Your people shall ponder and remember and think, spiritually think, not at a natural level, but let the Spirit Himself reveal areas of weakness, weapons of the devil, weapons of God, the equipment for overcoming in this glorious warfare. Lord, we pray that You will leave now Your very rich blessing on all Your people, for Christ's sake, Amen.

Notes

[1] This is our coffee/bookshop, now up and paid for. All the money came in months before the date of completion. The building's use has since been extended by the addition of a mezzanine floor.

[2] For further teaching on faith, see my *Reflections on the Gifts of the Spirit* (New Dawn Books, 1988), chapters 3 and 4, and *Christian Fundamentals* (New Dawn Books, 1991), chapters 10 and 11.

[3] This is not to suggest that other prayer meetings held in the church are less important or less powerful. Indeed some are quite phenomenal. At the time of preaching, however, the Monday early morning meeting had just started and was particularly in my mind.

[4] *Stookie:* (cf. *stucco*) Scots word meaning plaster cast or statue – humorously suggesting helpless disadvantage or passivity.

[5] Bruce Olson, *Bruchko* (New Wine Press; © 1973, 1978 by Creation House).

[6] This book is now published under the title *E.H. Taylor, A Modern Christian Mystic: Sayings and Recollections*.

[7] From Mrs Charles Cowman, *Streams in the Desert* vol. 3 (Marshall Pickering, 1968, reprinted 1990; © Cowman Publications, Inc., 1939, 1968 and 1990), reading for 21 December.

[8] This was at a disastrous time in 1993!

[9] One of Glasgow's main shopping precincts.

[10] A leader and founder member of the Struthers movement.

[11] Mary Black, whose story is told in *Christian Fundamentals*, chapter 4.

[12] An allusion to 1 Kings 17:11–13.

[13] Cowman, *Streams in the Desert* vol. 2 (Marshall Pickering, © Cowman Publications, Inc., 1966), reading for 10 November.

[14] See Amy Carmichael, *Gold Cord: The Story of a Fellowship* (Christian Literature Crusade, 1974), p. 241. For further detail of my own story see my *Reflections on the Gifts of the Spirit*, pp. 171–4.

Chapter 4

Deliverance

We move on directly to a key topic of our study.

Deliverance is a much misunderstood word, and in my view it is often incorrectly used. I wish first to divide the subject into two main sections, and very briefly touch on the first.

Physical Deliverance

Deliverance deals with the body as well as the spiritual part of man. And that, of course, involves healing: deliverance from illness, from disease. Now I have always tried to be totally balanced on this. I see in Scripture that there is healing, very definitely and very clearly. You find instruction given: for example,

> *Is any among you sick? let him call for the elders of the church; and let them pray over him, anointing him with oil in the name of the Lord: And the prayer of faith shall save him that is sick.* (James 5:14–15)

And it is in general God's will that His people be in health. But Scripture makes it equally clear that all were not healed. Epaphroditus was left sick at Miletum (2 Timothy 4:20). Paul had a thorn in the flesh, whether of a physical or a spiritual nature we are not told, but he was not healed of whatever it was, and he was told that God's grace was sufficient for him. He realized ultimately that this thorn in the flesh was a good thing for him: it was pressing him closer to the very heart of Christ. It first seemed a curse, but it ultimately brought blessing. I have observed through many years that there are people whom God heals miraculously and sometimes instantaneously, and there are other people, so far as I can judge equally good and maybe sometimes better, whom God does not heal, and who glorify Him from beds of suffering.

Let me make this very clear to you. One of the ladies who was deeply used in revival in Lewis was Barbara. I remember going to visit her, and I could only get an appointment by arrangement when she was sufficiently well to receive visitors. She ultimately spoke to me, between gasps of pain, of revival in time past and of some of the wonderful things that had happened. I went in to her room with the attitude of learning from a saint of God. I didn't go in with pride: 'I'm God's man for the hour, and I'm pentecostal, and you should be out of that sick bed and get up and glorify God.' I wouldn't have dared. I was in the presence of a saint, and a suffering saint.

She spoke about revival, and I sat and listened. 'Oh,' she said, 'revival: it is wonderful – for some people. But for those of us who carried the prayer burden, it was a terrible time. We weren't in the meetings; we were in a room apart, and as the burden of souls came on us time after time after time, it was as if we were being emptied and filled up again and again as children were being born, as souls were brought to God in another room.' A wonderful time – for some people. A time of deep, deep intercession and burden for others. I remember one of the men of that locality telling me, 'During the revival I was standing in a pub in Stornoway and was about to raise a glass to my lips when Barbara in spirit stood before me. I couldn't touch the drink, and I went home. As I was going through Barvas she stepped out from her house and I fell on my knees and was converted in the open street.'

Now Barbara suffered intense pain at the end of her days. Hudson Taylor's closing years, and Amy Carmichael's closing years, were in pain. Am I going to tell people like these that they should be healed and they are dishonouring God by not being healed? I think not. I recommend a book to you: *Charismatic Renewal*, and an article in it by Tom Smail, in which he shows that for some there is healing and there are others who have fellowship with the Lord Jesus in His suffering. And, you know, when Christ was enduring the pains of the cross, He wasn't being instantaneously healed as these pains came upon Him. He drank the cup to the last bitter drop: He suffered, and He died in suffering. There are two ways whereby you can glorify God. You can be instantaneously healed, with all the glory that that brings to God, or you can go through your own Gethsemane and Calvary and be identified with Christ in His cross. This is another but equally valid model. It may in fact be the higher honour.

Through the years God has been very gracious to us. We have seen many, many healings. I often ask audiences to indicate by standing if they have known miraculous healing, and large numbers normally do so.

George, in a nutshell, come and tell the people what God did for you.[1]

I suffered from manic depression, which I developed at the age of seventeen. It had worsened to such a stage that I lost my job because I was unable to work. I arrived home to Glasgow and went on the scrapheap. There was absolutely no hope for me, no future, and the psychiatrist who had been treating me had actually made me worse. Life seemed to be at an end, and in November of 1987 I was sitting in a communion service on a Sunday morning when during the time of prayer Mr Black came over and laid hands on me, and I knew at that point that the tide had turned.

Within two months I could say that I was completely
healed. All of the things that I was unable to do
before then, I was able to do in full measure. I took
up a university appointment in Manchester and
subsequently completed a PhD degree. From being a
manic depressive, I became completely well and have
been able to cope with what would normally be
considered very stressful situations. So the healing of
God was complete and full.

George has really abbreviated the story of his healing
this time! Let me fill in a few of the details. George had
taken his honours BSc and he was engaged in medical
research at Sheffield university. As he said, he found
himself on the scrapheap and could do nothing about it.
He suffered desperately. Then God touched him in a
moment of time, and when he went back to Sheffield he
completed his thesis within about two months. George
has subsequently been engaged in some of the most
advanced research in his field. He is now one of the fore-
most authorities in the world in certain aspects of that
work. When his professor (who was a Christian) saw him
on his return, he exclaimed, 'Now, Lord, let thy servant
depart in peace, for mine eyes have seen thy salvation.' He
had never expected such an outcome and realized he had
witnessed a miracle. Miracles of healing occur frequently
in our midst, and we can testify that God does deliver in
the physical realm, blessed be his Name.

Spiritual Deliverance

However, I do not want to major on healing. I want to
come to deliverance in the sense that most people understand the word. Let me say, first, that there is deliverance
from demon possession. Now I really mean possession,
where a person is indwelt and driven by an evil power,
having little if any control over certain actions. That is
deep possession, the kind where a person is thrown into a

fire, as you read in the gospels. And may I put this point in: a great part of the ministry of Christ lay in dealing with demoniacs. There was great emphasis on clearing demons out of individuals. Be aware of that. It is very strongly emphasized in the pages of the New Testament. We are not meeting that deep kind of possession every day, but I want to give you one example of fairly deep possession, or near possession. But before doing so, I want to make something clear, and this may be controversial. It is something which I would not have believed myself in my early stages as a Christian, and I am not putting it in merely to stir controversy. I am relating it as factual.

I believe that a person can be thoroughly converted and still have a demon. I believe that a person can be thoroughly converted, baptized in the Holy Spirit, and still have a demon. I believe a person can be converted, baptized in the Spirit and deeply used in the kingdom of God, and still have a demon. Now I know that this can put shutters up in some audiences right away. You may say, 'I don't believe that – how can that be?' I want you to be reasonable and bear with me for a moment. Supposing I said to you that I have a friend who is dying in hospital of a dread disease, but, thank God, he knows Christ, you wouldn't think that there was anything odd about a Christian dying of a dread disease. There would be no contradiction in terms. Such deaths happen to converted people. In other words, the body is in a desperate condition but it is still a temple of the Holy Spirit. And if you can accept this where the body and disease is concerned, why is it so difficult to accept that if one area of the spiritual being has been affected in time past by a demon gaining entrance and foothold, the person concerned may still be a child of God? It took me time to come to terms with this, and Miss Taylor, who was so deeply used in our movement, took even longer to come to terms with it. But ultimately we both realized the truth. There often is deliverance of genuinely committed Christians, and sometimes from things that they never knew they had. Before going on to our example I want first to cite two cases away from our own situation. These two cases are historic.

Celebrated Cases

One relates to Don Basham, a famous author and preacher, much used in charismatic circles. Coming from an Episcopalian background, he was thoroughly converted and baptized in the Holy Spirit. He became a leader in the charismatic movement and was teaching pentecostal doctrine. One day he realized that he was dealing with a demon inside him, and he explains in writing that there came upon him from time to time horror, devastating fear that incapacitated him seriously. He ultimately traced his condition back to a day when he was about eight or nine years old. His brother had been in charge of him and had taken him to see a horror film. From that hour a spirit of fear came upon that boy, that young man, that adult, manifesting itself from time to time. When it was upon him he was out of the game; he was devastated. And Don Basham, leader though he was, had to have deliverance. That spirit of fear was cast out as it was revealed, and he was able to function for God.[2]

The other case is that of an equally famous charismatic leader. He is still alive, having had tremendous influence in America and been much used in this country: Derek Prince. As an adult leader of the people of God he realized one day that the bad temper from which he suffered was irrational: it was beyond normal. He had to have deliverance. That evil spirit of temper was cast out of him and he was left a whole man.[3]

Friends, I have seen countless numbers of people delivered, and I assure you that most of those from whom I have seen demons cast out have been born-again men and women, because God's direction at this present time is first to the church: judgment must first begin at the house of God. Cleansing comes to the elect, and then it reaches out beyond the church. I assure you that from across the country, from all around they come in numbers for deliverance. Now all deliverance is not of the deepest kind, but the first I describe was deep.

Raymond

Raymond's case I can speak of because he has done so himself publicly.[4] His is an interesting story. He came to Christ and to us as the result of the death of a little daughter of about five, who succumbed to a very unusual disease. As Raymond looked on her in death he suddenly seemed to have an absolute conviction that unless he found God he would never see her again. He was devastated, and a friend brought him to our church. There was no particular movement in him to salvation in the early stages. But one night he said to me, 'I would like you to pray for me, because I have a drink problem.' I had not known he had a drink problem, I suppose because in popular parlance he could 'hold his liquor', and it showed not at all. Evidently he was drinking like a fish – a really amazing amount of liquor. He was prayed for, and in a moment of time was delivered from alcohol and from smoking, which he hadn't mentioned. So far as I am aware he never again touched a drop of alcohol or a cigarette. And he was still unsaved. I waited for about a fortnight, and then I asked him, 'Raymond, have you never thought of giving your life to Christ?'

'Yes,' he said, 'I'm going to get saved tomorrow night.'

'And what would be wrong with tonight?'

'Well, I have been running a crooked business, and I've got the books in my car to go to the accountant tomorrow to get my business straightened out. As soon as I get this sorted, I'm going to get converted.'

I said, 'Well, Raymond, if you genuinely mean to go right, God will accept that now; the intention is there. You don't need to postpone your salvation. Let's go into the kitchen' – no ornate palaces, just the kitchen.

He gave his life to Christ there on the spot. I laid hands

on him quietly, and he was wonderfully baptized in the Holy Spirit, speaking in tongues as the Spirit gave utterance. He landed on the floor, and I brought his friend in. We were delighted that he was through.

Now watch this: it is true; verifiable.

Some months passed, and I was dealing with that awful Bible reading in Romans chapter one where it lists gross sins. There was someone attending at that time whom I judged to be unclean and in need of deliverance. I didn't preach at him, but I didn't miss him in the preaching. And, you know, sometimes you are fishing for someone but it's another fish that takes the hook. It was Raymond who took the hook not on the ground of immorality but on the ground of demon trouble, and the other sat there regardless. Raymond had a terrible week. As he went home there were voices speaking: 'Don't go back there! It will kill you; don't go back there; don't go near that place again.' I can't remember all the close detail, but he had one fearful week. On the Saturday night he was not responding, but a friend persuaded him to come (reluctantly) for ministry. When he sat down beside me he said, 'I've got a demon.' I said, 'I don't think you've got any such thing, Raymond.' 'Oh, yes,' he said, 'I have.'

I said, 'Well, there's no point in arguing. We'll soon find out. Just wait a minute or two until I'm free in the vestry' – because I had to deal with someone else for deliverance who indeed received it that night. At the tail end of this deliverance I brought Raymond in. He got the fright of his life, because seeing a person being delivered can sometimes be quite scary. There Raymond sat, and I laid hands on him. Within seconds I knew he was right in his diagnosis and I was wrong. It was not just one demon: he had about seven screaming convulsions as they came out one by one. Indeed, it was about three months, I think, before he was totally clear. Now here was a man who had been wonderfully healed, genuinely saved, and **afterwards** delivered. As I investigated, I learned that he had lived a very bad life. You see, God can save the soul very simply.

With one touch on the hem of His garment, as it were, a man can pass from death to life. But that part of the being that has been so deeply affected by evil, where demons have had a foothold, may still have to be dealt with and evil entities driven out, and it takes the power of the living God to do that.

An Early Deliverance

I remember another case from my early days in this ministry. Pentecost had moved into a family and their connections, until about thirty of them were saved and baptized in the Spirit. Some were saved before I knew them but they then came into the baptism. There was a husband and wife who lived at a distance, but they too became interested. The man ultimately came into the area on holiday and was seeking salvation. I remember getting a call about a quarter to eleven one Sunday night, and I went round to where he stayed. He was desperate, and it is wonderful to help someone who is really desperate for salvation. It is lovely to lead them to Christ; it is not difficult. There he found salvation, and it was wonderful. I was about to let him go to share his joy with other members of the family, when I suddenly thought, 'No, I'll not. I'll pray for his baptism in the Spirit.' And I laid hands on him. Having less experience then than now, I got quite a shock. Suddenly his face was distorted with agony. I thought, 'If some of my evangelical friends saw me now, they would have me chased out of the country. Here's a man just saved and so recently reflecting the glory of God, and now he is in a state of absolute anguish.' However, I continued to pray, and he told me later it was as though something inside him was rent in two and he was torn apart. The effects of a lifetime of sin were dealt with, and he experienced deep deliverance. That man was already converted, but to be fully free he had to experience deliverance. He was then filled with the Holy Spirit, rejoicing in God, and glory filled the temple.

Again shall I put it to you? If you can accept that a man may die with a fearful disease and still be a true Christian, surely he may be a true Christian and still require to have demons dealt with. Now I don't expect all of you to accept that at a first hearing, but I assure you that the evidence for it is absolutely undeniable.

Pauline

A testimony from Pauline corroborates this teaching.[5]

My deliverance happened about thirteen and a half years ago. I had been saved and baptized in the Spirit and was going on with God. From the moment of my baptism there was never a point where I didn't do what I felt God was asking. I wasn't the type of person who could sweep things under the carpet if I felt God had spoken. So it was against that background that this happened. I knew virtually nothing about deliverance; I had maybe suspected once that I had heard somebody being prayed with for deliverance, but there were two shut doors between me and what was happening, and I was quite pleased! I never for a moment – and I do want to underline this – I never for a moment thought that I was in any kind of need of deliverance. Never. If anybody had told me, I would have been absolutely terrified at that time, and I would have thought, 'Me? Not me!' I mean, I was quite a good and respectable kind of person, and to think that I would actually need deliverance was something that never entered my head! It came as an absolute shock to my system. But it completely changed my life.

One night during a prayer time at our church camp I became aware that I just couldn't get through to God in the way I normally did. On the way out of the meeting I spoke to Mr Black and said, 'You know, I just felt I couldn't get through to God.' Now it wasn't a big issue; it was as though I had met an invisible barrier, and I was intending to go to my bed and hope that when I got up in the morning things would be OK. I did get up in the morning and they were OK – but not in quite the way I had been supposing.

Mr Black said, 'Well, we'll just pray.'

I know from what he said at the time that he didn't expect what happened any more than I did. As we began to pray (and I saw this visually), it was as though I was in an underground tunnel, something like an animal might live in. It would have about six feet head-room and it was not terribly wide. Standing in front of me and just slightly to my left, I saw Christ. And it wasn't what He looked like that really impressed me; it was what He was. I became aware of a power that I had never known existed. Up until that point I had thought of presidents and prime ministers and world political leaders as the people who had power. In that moment I became aware of a power far greater than all the powers of earth put together. I knew with absolute assurance you couldn't argue with that power. You could not argue with that Person who was standing there. I felt the absolute strength that was in Him – and it was coming against something in me. I knew very quickly that I had a choice to make. I could either side with Christ, or I could try to fight against Him. But I knew that was not really an option. In a moment of time I made my decision to be on Christ's side. I actually felt then what the demon was feeling. I knew there was something in me which needed to go – and I felt as though I was being catapulted up the tunnel at about a hundred miles an hour. Looking back, I now realize the demon could not stand that presence of God, and what it felt was communicated to me. It absolutely fled and I was left totally free.

It was quite traumatic, though; I have to be honest. There was a side to it that was not nice. I screamed in

a way that I never have either before or since. But I
found that the experience completely changed my life.
From that point on I found I was able to make
decisions for God that I would previously have
wanted to make but been unable. I would only have
been able to go so far: something would have held me
back, particularly in the line of holiness and sanctification. As teaching was being given, I knew, I just
knew the type of life that God wanted me to live. I
saw it, and I knew that in this twentieth century,
when people were being involved in immorality, even
Christians living a wrong way, it didn't need to be
like that. I knew that there was power in Jesus Christ
to deliver a soul and keep one and enable one to live
in a completely different dimension, a completely
different realm.

And it has been like that ever since. That was thirteen and a half years ago: so the experience has stood
the test of time. Life has completely changed since
then. There is a tremendous freedom in spiritual life.
A number of years ago as I was praying I became
aware that there was a wonderful freedom up higher.
It was just like going up into a realm where there was
nothing at all to hold you down to earth, and you
were completely free. I have felt that over the years. I
have been tremendously grateful to God for that
sense of freedom, for the sense that there is nothing
that needs to hold you bound, or to hold you down to
earth.

That strength, that power of Christ that I saw thirteen and a half years ago in the tunnel, came before
me a few years ago. And this time something of it
actually came inside. I remember becoming aware:
'It's not just out there any more, it's not out there
coming against something in me, but something of
that essential strength and iron has actually come
inside me.' This has strengthened as the years have
gone on. I do thank God for what He has done. One

side of the experience was not pleasant; I have to underline that. But, you know, I would go through it all again. If I thought today that there was something needing dealt with, I would be the first to go for prayer. I know the difference that it has made in my life, and there is no turning back, none at all. As the chorus goes,

> I have decided to follow Jesus,
> No turning back.

Go on a little, Pauline. Tell a little of what you have seen after the strength came (because Pauline has become involved in deliverance ministry).

Three things happened, really, over the same period of time, maybe about five or six years ago. I became aware of tremendous freedom as I prayed. I often say I know what it must be like for an eagle to be soaring through the sky. There is a tremendous sense that there is nothing, but nothing, to hold you down to earth. That happened. The second thing was the revelation of the strength of Christ actually coming inside: the two things happened within a day or two of each other.

But you know, something else happened, and this, again, was a turning point in my life. Up until that point, I really thought that most Christians were living quite good, victorious lives. Now I was quite naive in this; it was almost as though I was in a dream world. I thought that Christians only needed to know what to do and they would do it, and also that they were generally living in freedom. And, you know, I remember at that time when the sense of freedom and the power of Christ came in my own life, it was as though God opened my eyes, and I had a sense of wakening up. For the first time in my life I saw a truth that in one way I wish I hadn't seen. I wish that what I saw was not true. I became aware that what I had thought for years about Christians living victorious lives was mistaken. God showed me Christians – not non-Christians, but the Christian church – with lives that had pain, that had brokenness, that needed deliverance. The needs were all there inside. And I knew that instead of living in that realm of freedom and victory where they knew the power of the overcoming Christ, that wasn't the case.

From that moment I found that what I saw in spirit was the truth; I actually saw it in reality. From that point I began to be used in deliverance, and Mr Black took me in a team to many different parts of the country where he went to minister. Sometimes with others and sometimes alone, I have been from the north of Scotland to the south of England and into Wales. And I would love to be able to say the picture is different, that the picture is good. But no matter where I have been over the years, there is one fact that emerges again and again, and it is that people are not free. Now that is just a fact. Many Christians, born again, baptized in the Holy Spirit, working for God as much as they are able, find at the end of the day that there are things binding them: fears, worries, oppressions, demons of one kind and another. By and large the Christian church is not free. That's the negative side. But I tell you, the good side is that as we have gone around there have been those that God has put His hand upon, those who have been hungry for freedom, those who have known there is something else and have found it. There **is** a realm of freedom, there **is** a realm of overcoming, and I do thank God that I have seen many, many lives over the last five or six years whom God has set free. It is a privilege. I do feel this is part of the work of God in these days. There is the work amongst the unsaved, and we mustn't neglect that. But there is a work that God is doing within the hearts of men and women in His own church, and I thank God to have been a part of that.

I should explain that there is a team of about ten or a dozen of us who have come into this line of ministry. I used to go alone, but I found that when I preached a full-scale message on deliverance normally a third to a half of an audience would come for ministry. Indeed I quite often warn the people organizing that type of meeting that there is likely to be that kind of response. Sometimes it goes up to ninety per cent, and I have known it be a hundred per cent. You will realize why I now take a team with me.

Now some of you may be wondering about points which are emerging. Let me explain. While there is deliverance of the deep kind that I mentioned in connection with Raymond, there are many other kinds that are not so intense. You will find, for example, that through immorality in its various shades, or through involvement in the occult, demons get entrance and have to be driven out. I find also that many people suffer from phobias, and these are similarly dealt with. I frequently state publicly that almost all suffering from phobias are likely to be set free through deliverance ministry and usually in about two minutes flat, and that permanently. The phobias really do not return. Case after case of that can be given.

You will also find that there are people who are suffering from wounded spirits. They have been wronged, but the pain has gone in to a point where an entity has got a grip. This can also happen with excessive grief. I believe that initially we all have a covering, a guard; but if that guard is broken, let it be with hysteria, bad temper, or loss of control, we leave an avenue for invasion. Demons can get an entrance along many different lines. Immorality is a very highway for entrance; dabbling in the occult is another. We find that the entities are of various kinds, and as a situation is probed they become evident, and there is power in Christ to cast them out.

Shall we listen to evidence?

Jimmy

Jimmy Lunan, violent man and protestant gang leader in a sectarian-riven town, married Maureen of Catholic background, with the effect that you can imagine on both families.[6] They both found Christ as Saviour and were both baptized in the Holy Spirit. Jimmy was healed in a moment of time of rheumatoid arthritis, having been in awful pain for years, finding no relief except in cold baths. He came to our house on an occasion when I wasn't there, and my daughter Mary prayed. She had an inner vision of Christ as she did so; she saw His hands open and turn upwards. She said, 'Jimmy, open your hands.' The pain had left him by then, but he knew that it could take days to loosen his fingers. He said that he couldn't open his hands – but to his amazement he did open them. He was healed in a moment of time. And he has never had another twinge of arthritis.[7]

The same Jimmy came into our church bookshop one day limping and hopping on one foot. His wife Maureen was with him. He was suffering from a Pott's fracture. He had not gone to hospital and was in a bad state. An ambulance driver present at the time said, 'You'll be in trouble, Jimmy, when they get you into hospital. You neglected that. You're in real trouble.'

Maureen said, 'He's come to be healed.' I thought (not over-brimming with faith), 'Wonderful . . . ' We went into the kitchen next door. Jimmy sat in a chair, and I squatted beside him. When I put my hands on his ankle, it was as though a bolt came from heaven. His ankle was healed, he put his shoe on, got up and walked into the next room. With some delay as I eased myself up from the floor, I followed him. You should have seen the faces of the folk present. One of them at first would not – could not – believe it. And do you know, he did a jig up and down that shop, danced up and down it. Meantime I was thinking (because I'm an old Scotsman), 'Everybody wants to be healed, and sometimes there is wishful thinking.' I'm maybe naturally a bit of a sceptic: a terrible admission for a leader to make! But I thought to myself, 'I'll watch when nobody's looking at him to see if he starts limping again, and I'll watch him walking away along the lane outside.' I had a long time to wait, because he and Maureen started doing the dishes and stayed about two hours in the shop, and there he was dancing up and down and hopping from foot to foot: never a twinge. And I looked after him as he walked along the lane as sprightly as a bird!

When they left their house in the tenement that morning, a neighbour said, 'Going to the hospital, Jimmy?'

'No,' he said, 'I'm going to get healed. I'm going to the church to get my ankle healed.'

'Ha,' the neighbour said, 'that'll be right.'

Maureen replied, 'We'll be back at such-and-such a time: you wait and you'll see.' And sure enough, he went back totally healed, and the neighbour did see.

You'll say, 'Well, that's wonderful. Saved, baptized in the Spirit, wonderfully, miraculously healed!'

Not only that; both Jimmy and Maureen had a wonderful vision of angels.[8]

But he knew, and my daughter Grace knew, that deep down there was demon trouble. You say, 'After all that?' Yes, after all that.

He had been a very violent man – and I really mean violent: it wasn't a case of 'tippytappy'.[9] A spirit of deep violence was now surfacing. Half-a-dozen of us went into the vestry. And he was a gentleman; he didn't want to harm anybody, but he knew the danger as this evil power became manifest and began to try to get control as it was being dealt with. But it was (or rather they were), cast out.

He said a very interesting thing when he came back to a normal state: 'You know, I could see what the demon was doing. It was looking round to see if there was anybody in that group uncovered, whom it could attack or enter. People could have been in real danger from it. Fortunately everybody was covered, not all equally deeply, but all covered.'

Mark that. I remember speaking to a woman greatly used of God without our circles altogether, working with the oppressed and the child-abused, working strongly against Satan. She told me that when she comes against some of the people deeply involved in the occult, immediately the possessing demons look to see if there is a point of weakness in her which might be exploited. It is dangerous to be involved in this kind of work without the covering of God, without the call of God, without holiness.

Maureen

After Maureen was saved and baptized in the Spirit, and after she had seen a vision of angels,[10] she came to me one day, and she wanted rid of what she called the box. I will leave her to tell her own story.

I was saved and baptized, and God was moving in and through my life. But at one of the camps the word was coming, and the word was like very fresh air for my lungs, and food – but I thought, 'I can't cope with this, because what's coming is not getting in; I'm not getting fed.' I just felt I couldn't breathe properly. So I went away and got before God, and I said, 'God, show me clearly what's wrong with me.' I just sat quietly and closed my eyes, and I saw something like a steel chest. At that point God transported me back in spirit to the night that I got saved, when the lady [Jean Darnall] who had led me to Christ had said to me, 'You've been hurt so deeply and badly, but Christ has come to take it away.' I had taken her word on it literally, and I thought, 'Right, it's done.' God in His grace and His mercy accepted me as I was then. But when I saw that steel chest, the two things came together. Christ had come to me earlier but there was more to be fulfilled of His promise.

He said, 'Now I want to deal with it.' So I went to Mr Black and said, 'Mr Black, I've got a box inside me!'

He said, 'Right, we'll let Christ open it.'

I said, 'But I don't know if I want to see what's in it, because I know that everything, all my hurts, all my fears, everything that I could not cope with and I couldn't face I stuck in that box, and the lid is tight. I can't open it; I don't know if I want it opened.'

He said, 'Let Christ open it.'

So Pauline and Mr Black started praying with me. As soon as they put their hands on my back, Christ was standing in front of me. And He lifted the box – He didn't look at it Himself; He opened it. I knew I was pulling away. But He said, 'Look.' And when I looked in, I saw it all – it was just a **mangle**. And I started screaming. That's it, it was a mangle: it was like spaghetti! As soon as that was over, He just closed the box and threw it away. I could see what was happening spiritually.

Mr Black said, 'Just stay where you are, Maureen, He's going to pour in His healing balm.' I sat there. I saw what was like a clear transparent tube, and there was no bottom. It was clear right down, and I thought, 'I'm empty.' For the first time in my life I could sit there and say, 'I am empty.' There was just nothing binding or hurting. And I could see the healing balm and the light. It flowed in from head to foot, and when it hit down to my feet I started laughing. I remembered how from a very early age I had no covering. I had seen demons and known family troubles; I had been in the midst of demonic things, but I had no cover. I didn't know how to be protected, and a lot of the hurt of that had been in the box. But when I saw Christ, it was sorted. You may think on the Crucified as a weakling, but when I saw that risen Christ I saw power and strength, and what had flowed in was cleanness and purity. I just couldn't get over the fact: 'He's a risen Saviour! He's not a weakling, but He's a risen Saviour.' The power came in and I started laughing. It was really powerful. And all Mr Black said was, 'Aye, laugh away, hen, because there's too many tears in the world today!'

The detail of the conversation about the box was quite amusing.

I said, 'What's wrong, Maureen?'

She said, 'It's the box.'

I thought, 'What do you mean, the box?' Maybe she had been watching television and seeing something she shouldn't have been looking at!

'No, no,' she said, 'it's not that; it's a box, it's inside me.' And it had to be opened and emptied and the whole thing thrown away.

Now these are really very typical examples that I have given. Any of you who are interested in the theoretic side of this will find it in *Christ the Deliverer*. For present purposes I want to touch on three other areas.

Deliverance from Phobias

The first area is that of phobias. Graham, will you tell your story?

I have been set free from a number of phobias, some of which many guys wouldn't like to admit to. The biggest one was fear of spiders, from an early age. Once when I had been in a bath spiders had dropped on top of me and crawled up my back, whereupon I had jumped out the bath and screamed a good deal. Ever since then I had a real fear of spiders. One night praying by myself in my room I asked Christ to set me free from that fear, and He did. Christ came and He set me completely free from it.

Another one around the same time was fear of darkness. This had been with me from a very young age. Again, I was in my room by myself; my folks were away for the weekend and I was sitting praying, and simply asked Christ to come in. Again I felt Him coming, and I had an experience of light where after a while I opened my eyes, and my room was filled with the light of Christ. There were no lights on in my room, and it was about two o'clock in the morning. Christ was really there; the room was just thick with His presence. These things happened about four and a half years ago, and I have never had a fear of spiders or of darkness since; Christ has totally set me free. Praise His name.

Let me now give you a typical example and show you the theory and the outworking. One of our ladies had a fear of fire from childhood, when a matchbox had exploded in her hand. She dreaded even pictures of fire. She came for ministry, and it is not the case itself so much as the way of dealing with it that I want to bring to you. It is essential to get to the very root of these problems; it is not enough to deal superficially.

I remember saying to her 'Go into the Spirit, Linda,' which she did; she went into tongues and praised God. I said, 'I want you to picture yourself in a burning house. You are in the bottom flat and the doors are locked, and it becomes a raging inferno.' I could see the agony rising in her face. And I did this deliberately; I have to do this, to get right to the bottom of it.

Just as it got to its peak, I said, 'Now the Lord Jesus is beside you. Go to the door.'

She told me later, 'I didn't need to go to the door. In the moment that Christ stood there all the flames went out and He lifted me right out.' She was totally set free, and she said, 'Not only was I set free, but other things were dealt with – there were various bitternesses and resentments, and they were all taken in one swoop.'

That is an entirely typical example; I could give you many, many others. And I can tell you that no matter what your phobia is, Christ can set you free, be it fear of birds, fear of flying, fear of whatever: snakes, spiders, height, depth, drowning – oh, the phobias are manifold, and He heals them all, wonderfully, gloriously. I have stood in an audience of hundreds and claimed that there was never a failure. (Actually, two people did ultimately tell me that there had not been success in their case.) But across the country, across the board, success is almost a hundred per cent.

I remember asking one of my doctor friends how our method of dealing with these matters compared with the way in which the medical profession dealt with them. I got quite a cynical answer.

'Well,' he said, 'often it takes about a year to treat a phobia, and sometimes nothing very much happens' – whereas when it is done directly by God, healing can happen in a moment of time, and it is permanent.

Deliverance from the Occult

I would like to report of up-to-date matters. Very recently I had a phone call from a minister who was in touch with someone in real need. The lady had been told by one of the spiritual leaders she was working with that she was all right, but she knew deep down that this was not so. About three weeks ago she came with my minister friend for ministry. Diana (see chapter 2) was present on the occasion, and I want her to tell a little of what happened. The lady saw Christ, and her experience has deeply affected others with whom she is involved. I would like Diana to supply background detail.

About a fortnight ago, one Tuesday night, Mr Black asked Grace and me to come through to the Glasgow Tuesday night meeting. There was a girl there from another church who was seeking ministry. In her own fellowship there was someone who had some level of discernment, who had indicated that she was in need of deliverance, and had told her with great accuracy things about herself that nobody else knew. Basically there had been an occult spirit working in her life, and she had been very involved in the occult in her childhood. I think circumstances had driven her towards that, and in some ways she had been a very lonely person. She came for ministry, and Christ met her need in a very beautiful way. It was quite difficult for a time before she got fully through and was fully delivered. But there came a point when Christ Himself came, and as she went right out to God He set her free, and the demon was driven out. Straight away she said she felt totally different: she felt very light, as though something had completely gone from her. She burst into real joy and laughter at the end of the experience. There was such a sense of freedom and relief that the whole thing was dealt with, and she knew it herself. Evidently the following day she had a very deep experience: Christ drew very close and revealed Himself to her, and I think since then she hasn't stopped talking about what happened, and what Christ has done for her. Someone who is in touch with her has spoken of seeing a tremendous change since that occasion. We witnessed the real delivering power of Christ.

Diana and Grace are particularly used against the occult (see chapter 2). I now delegate a good deal, and these two often operate on their own. It is very encouraging to observe the fruits of their ministry, which is becoming increasingly known. They are called from time to time to deal with particularly difficult cases. Both are gentle people, but when they come under the anointing in that particular ministry there is a transformation which is quite remarkable.

The Pearl

I now want a contribution from Grace on an unusual aspect of deliverance. There is a very sweet ministry in which she has been used from time to time, and in this connection I have asked her to speak about 'the pearl'.

I became very sharply aware a number of years ago of a line of help that was really needed in the church of Christ. I began to realize first of all that there were lives in our midst who were in need of very deep inner healing, even in some cases where there had already been deliverance, or in others where deliverance had not been needed but there were areas still closed to God. Lives could be closed, not necessarily because there was any dark power there, but because there had been deep, deep levels of hurt. I found whenever I started to speak on this line that more and more response came. I remember once speaking to a mature Christian who revealed a level of hurt that they had never been able to speak about before. They began to cry as they spoke about it. And the presence of God came into the room to heal the thing that had blighted their life and their personality. It made me become terribly aware of just how deep this kind of thing could go. I began to speak about it and found it brought a deep response. One particular life came to me, and I have used her case again and again because it makes the truth so clear and it is the easiest way of illustrating it.

She came and said that she had really tried to put into practice the teaching I had given about bringing every hurt deep or small to the Lord Jesus Christ, and letting Him be the healing, letting Him be the defence, letting Him be the shield, rather than building a wall of defence which becomes a hardness and eventually a barrier that also keeps God out of the deepest, most feeling part of our being and of our spirit. She had tried to do this and found that it was really working, until as she continued in the path, Christ began to probe the deep level of her being where there was hurt that had never healed and she was afraid to look at: it was so deep, and it had come into her life so early. It took quite a long time; it was over a period of weeks that she found herself opening that deeper part of her being to Christ. He began to come into it, but the healing was not complete. I knew that she wasn't right through as deeply to God as He had always wanted her to be, and she knew it too. But there came a night when the matter came to a head. When we went to pray, by a miracle, by the power of the Holy Spirit, that part in her opened fully to God. She said afterwards it was as though He took her back in time, and showed her the very first time this level of hurt had come into her being, inflicted by another. He took her right back to that point, and at that point asked her to forgive that one. And in the light of Calvary (it was a miracle) she was able to do it. You know, I found it hard to say these words to her, 'Will you forgive?' because I myself found it hard to forgive what had been done to her, and I couldn't have asked her of myself; it was only Christ who could. She said, 'Oh, yes.' And then He asked her, 'Will you love that one?' And the love of Christ exploded inside her – His love for her – and then His love through her exploded to that one. It was really beautiful. She said afterwards she hadn't known that love like that existed. She knew then that Christ loved her and she loved Him.

And I became aware that we can build a barrier the way an oyster makes a pearl, which in one way is quite a beautiful thing. The pearl is its defence against the intruding grain of sand that has caused a wound. But the pearl is hard. So often we build these hardnesses, these barriers, to defend us (understandably) against hurt. Often it is people who are quite strong who suffer the most this way: they carry the hurt inside instead of bringing it to Christ to be healed. And it has to be all melted away and broken up for Christ to get in at the very deepest level of our being and take residence there. He becomes our shield and our defence, and He is the perfect one. No matter how strong we are, how independent, no matter how strong the barriers are that we build against other people hurting us, there is always a chink, there is always somebody that somehow can catch us off guard and get through. I have found that Christ is the only perfect, impenetrable barrier against any hurt and cruel arrow that the wicked one would send (and he knows our vulnerable points). Christ is the only sure defence. Nothing ever gets past Him. Blessed be His Name.

To round off this section: The term **Deliverance** can be applied to the healing of the body or the mind and to the expulsion of demons from our spirits. Possession may be very deep or fairly light. There are a number of areas in which there is a need for deliverance – immorality in its various forms, involvement with the occult, bondage resulting from unhealed wounds from earlier life, fear as a thing in itself unrelated to specific issues, phobias in general, grief that has gone too deep, haunted houses.

In all cases where there has been a penetration of the covering that is God-appointed for mankind generally, there is danger. When this has been broken through and entities have gained entrance, Christ can wholly and totally deliver and put a defence back in position. Remember also that these are negative sides of deliverance: these relate to **deliverance out of**. There is the glorious other side: **freeing into**. Because so many people have never known anything higher than normal living, they don't realize the freedom that there is for the sons and daughters of God. For so many it is not deliverance out of, but emancipation into.

If ... the Son shall make you free, ye shall be free indeed. (John 8:36)

I came that they may have life, and may have it abundantly. (John 10:10)

I believe that a New Testament Christian should be like an exploding bomb. You remember those fireworks known as zigzags that we used to have: they exploded all over the place. The New Testament Christians thrown out of Jerusalem went exploding all across the land. No matter where these early Christians went, they took life with them. They lit fires wherever they went. They were full of the Holy Ghost, and this had a powerful effect.

A New Testament Christian is so different from many of us. They had power, they loved not their lives, they did not count them dear to themselves; they carried the word of life; they would not obey man rather than God, and they were prepared to die for their faith: full of power like Stephen and dying glorious deaths. That is the picture of a New Testament Christian. And I tell you that the Pentecostal church, if I may come right close to home, is not measuring up to the New Testament church in so many cases. There is no royal road of safety. You can have a blazing movement today that is a dying wimp in a generation. There needs to be the living on the sharp edge from generation to generation. And the fire goes out very quickly unless we live there. But we can live there, and it is the mind and will of God that we should live there.

To what extent are you affecting your generation? To what extent are you showing forth the Lord Jesus? Is there a fire and a drive within you that will not let you go? If not, then there should be. And let's make no mistake about it. If the results are not there there is something wrong. Now I mean results not just in terms of numbers, but results in spiritual life. Are we Christ-men and Christ-women in our generation? Do others feel the power and the presence and the fragrance of Jesus as they meet us? If

127

not, why not? If not, we have fallen short. For that too we shall give an answer before the throne of God one day. Provision is made for us every one in the cross and in the resurrection of Jesus. What have we done for Christ? What are we doing for Christ? What will we do for Christ?

Notes

[1] The story of George Marshall's healing appears in greater detail in my *Christ the Deliverer*, pp. 56–9.

[2] For a fuller account of his deliverance from a spirit of fear, see Don Basham, *Deliver Us From Evil* (Hodder & Stoughton, 1973), chapter 15.

[3] *Ibid*, chapter 8.

[4] His story also appears in my *Reflections on the Gifts of the Spirit*, pp. 117–8.

[5] For Pauline Anderson's account of her conversion and subsequent life, see my book *The Incomparable Christ*, (New Dawn Books, 1989), pp. 153–71.

[6] A comprehensive account of Jimmy Lunan's story is given in my book *The Baptism of the Spirit and Its Effects* (New Dawn Books, 1994), chapter 14.

[7] For a fascinating account of the detail of this healing, see *Christ the Deliverer*, chapter 9.

[8] See *Christ the Deliverer*, appendix 3.

[9] For a long time I never knew the full detail of Jimmy's violent lifestyle, and I did not ask him. But it has since emerged and is recorded in *The Baptism in the Spirit and Its Effects*.

[10] See preceding note.

Chapter 5

War in the Heavenlies

Prayer: Lord our God, we pray that as we come into the next stage of our studies You will be with us. It is new ground, Lord, and we want to be careful for the direction of Your Spirit, not to be too academic and yet to be sufficiently so. Lord, help, we pray, for the Lord Jesus Christ's sake, for we need it. Amen.

For our wrestling is not against flesh and blood, but against the principalities, against the powers, against the world-rulers of this darkness, against the spiritual hosts of wickedness in the heavenly places.

(Ephesians 6:12)

Various terms for evil powers are used in the New Testament, e.g. principalities, powers, thrones, dominions, princes of wickedness, and many others. I believe that there is a hierarchy, and there are varying views of just what that hierarchy is.

It is generally held that whereas God is omnipresent, the devil is not, and that the latter delegates authority to his underlings, but there is no clear scriptural reference which can allow us to be dogmatic in our arranging of the hierarchy. We come to a speculative sphere, and when I am speculating I always like to say so. Much teaching and preaching is authoritative, but there is a place for speculation, and this should be recognized. We do know that there are various orders in the kingdom of darkness, but exactly how they relate to each other we are not certain. In a reading below, a Nigerian who had once been very deeply involved in witchcraft indicated the number of demon princes operating under him, each of whom governed an area through six hundred lesser demons. You may say we only have his word for that. But my own impression is that the world is greatly peopled with demon powers, and also I believe by angelic powers. I believe there is scriptural warrant for such a view.

One of the scriptures that has set people thinking deeply in this whole realm is found in the tenth chapter of the book of Daniel.

Daniel and the Prince of Persia

Let me summarize. There was a time when Daniel set his face to find God in a particular matter, and he fasted for twenty-one days. At the end of that time a messenger came and informed him that from the time he started to pray his request had been heard and granted, but the messenger who had been sent to him had been withstood by the prince of the power of Persia, and for twenty-one days the message had not got through. Here you have a situation where God Himself dispatches a messenger, that messenger is thwarted and opposed by an evil power, and it is twenty-one days before the message arrives. I believe that that battle was in the heavenlies, but it was also fought out through the body of Daniel, and if Daniel had succumbed and given up his fast and his prayer before God's appointed time, I do not believe that the messenger would have got through or the message been delivered. Here was a man of God moving by the direction of God and becoming a battlefield for these immense powers. The battle, I take it, was won on earth and recorded in heaven. Whichever way you look at it, there seems to have been an involvement and a connection between the two realms –

battle in the heavenlies and overcoming on the earth level.

Scholars, of course, have been aware of that part of Scripture for a long time. It is not a new discovery. But it has come into great prominence in more recent times, and that is partly because of experience building up in the actual spiritual battlefield. Where men and women of God have been deeply used in battling with evil power, that scripture has become tremendously significant. As a result of my own study, together with personal experience, I know that you do not fight the war at the periphery: the war must be fought at the centre, always.

Binding the Strong Man

I learned that principle in a comparatively small way in the early days in open-air work. I led an open-air on Saturday nights in Greenock from eleven o'clock until after midnight, when the pubs and picture houses were scaling. On Sundays we met from about ten o'clock. It was estimated that hundreds of people gathered for the meetings, and God was with us in power.

One day in the local library I came on something heretical. I wanted to know about the matter so that I would be able to confute it. In the pride of my young heart I did not realize that I was being dangerously affected as I read. One should never move other than with God in these matters. I could read that kind of thing today, and it wouldn't have the slightest effect on me, but at that time it badly affected my spirit.

The open-air came. Normally I could hardly get people off the platform; they were all wanting up, and sometimes the power of God was so great that they would say, 'Oh, I never felt anything like that in my life; I could have preached all night.' I would say, 'Well, you made an attempt, but you're not getting preaching all night. There are a whole lot of other people wanting to preach all night.

So down you come!' and I would pull their coat tails and down they came.

But that night I was in darkness; I was cut off from God. And would you believe it: nobody wanted to preach that night. 'Oh, no, I'm not in good form tonight. Don't ask me – don't ask me.' **But nobody** wanted to preach that night! And I suddenly realized that when the centre collapses the periphery folds. I realized my responsibility before God to be in a right condition and I quickly learned that when God sorts the matter He doesn't sort it at the periphery first; He sorts it at the centre. Learn this rule, for it is a rule of spiritual life: Christ Himself taught it. He said very clearly: you cannot destroy the strong man's possession until you bind the strong man. When he is bound then you can destroy his goods. Contrast our own foolish strategies. What do we do? We attack Satan's kingdom at the periphery and pick off a soul here and there, but leave the seat of his power untouched. I believe a day is coming when God will use his intercessors to deal with the corruption and the power at the centre of the opposition, and bind the powers at the centre. When these are broken, blessing flows in floods.

There are people who go deeply into the spiritual world and become aware of satanic strategy and fight at a deep level. They have supernatural knowledge. Many of you will know of Miss E.H. Taylor. She was a seer, and she knew God at great depth. As a headmaster, one day I suddenly found myself in real trouble in Greenock High School. There was a danger of a case coming against me through a very ill-disposed man, and she gave me early warning: she could see a dark cloud above the school. There was prayer covering and the danger was evaded. I had this kind of experience with both Miss Taylor and the late Mary MacLean of Lewis.[1] They both had very accurate knowledge. The same was true of the praying women of Barvas where the late Duncan Campbell was concerned: when he went in to see Peggy for the first time she said, 'Yes, you are God's servant after all.' He said,

'But you don't know me; you have never seen me.' 'Oh, yes,' she said, 'I have seen you.' And she named a day on which, she said, 'the devil tried to kill you'. She went on to say that at a particular hour in the afternoon 'the precious blood of Jesus came between you and him and you were saved'. He had been on his motor bike and almost involved in what could have been a fatal accident on that day at that hour. 'But', she said, 'the precious blood of Jesus came between you and him.'

Miss Taylor was like that. I remember one Saturday I was in real trouble – trouble that nobody knew about except me. I knew that the devil had made a toss for my soul. I was in great danger, but by God's grace I didn't go down. I knew I had had a narrow escape and I also felt I could take no credit to myself.

The next time Miss Taylor saw me she said, 'What were you doing at two o'clock last Saturday?' I evaded answering, and she continued, 'Because at that point the devil tried to get your soul. He wanted to finish you.' I no doubt looked intelligent and thoughtful, and I said never a word, because I didn't want her to know anything about what had happened. I didn't want anybody to know anything about it. And this may not be to my credit, but not for many years did I tell her that something significant happened on that day – and not even then did I tell her what it was. At that hour I had been in dreadful jeopardy, and she knew it. She was a woman of that kind.

Read the Lewis revival story. It is wonderful. Meet the old ladies who knew the mind of God and could tell Mr Campbell where to go on a particular occasion: 'You will go there.' He said, 'But I've not been invited there.' 'Oh, yes, God wants you to go there.' 'Well,' he said, 'we'll pray about it' – and prayer is often the last resort of the disobedient. They bowed, and she prayed: 'Lord, I have given this man the message you gave me, but he doesn't appear to be prepared to obey it. Lord, give this man wisdom.' I can just imagine him getting up and scratching his head a bit and saying, 'Well, I suppose I'd better go.'

'Yes,' she said, 'you'd better go. And you'll not be preaching for fifteen minutes before the Lord will give you seven souls.' When he got to the village they were waiting for him in that supernatural way that happens in revival. He had to preach from outside the house to the people inside. He had not been preaching for fifteen minutes before someone came to squeeze him in, and he found there were seven men lying on the floor: not six, not eight, but seven, every one of whom rose born again by the power of the living God. Mark the innerness of knowledge which the praying women had.[2]

A Transformed School

I want to give you another example from earlier days which involved Miss Taylor. I had been appointed to my first post as headmaster of the Mount School, and the school was in very bad condition. There had been eighty-four offences through the courts in the six months prior to my arrival. There was rioting, there was vandalism, there were protection rackets, there was thuggery by the square yard. And Miss Taylor, with vision, said, 'You know, this is going to become one of the crack schools of Scotland.' These were her words: a crack school. And I tell you, there was nobody in the whole country who would have believed it at that point. When I went in there I felt as though an evil beast was stalking the corridors. I have never forgotten this. There was real crime, violence, horrible things happening. And I felt something come over me, and God gave me the word:

> *I will make your forehead as adamant against their foreheads.*   (cf. Ezekiel 3:8–9)

The iron of God came into me, and without giving you the sordid details let me simply say that the evil in that school was crushed within about a fortnight to three weeks, powerfully and effectively and permanently broken. In the corresponding six months of the following year the number of criminal cases was down from eighty-four to sixteen. Thereafter it virtually disappeared. And it was the iron of God that did it.

So great was the effect that the crime figures for Greenock began to go against the national trend. The police investigated this and found that it was the Mount figures that tipped the balance.

Psychologists became interested and came to ask questions. I am not sure that they were too keen on what they learned about the need for firm discipline. I should say that the firm discipline was accompanied by real opportunity for pupils to have a great deal of valuable outdoor activity – which at that time was comparatively new.

I had no illusions that these methods reformed the hard criminal core. When general discipline is slack that core exercises an undue influence. It attracts to itself a number far greater than itself. It becomes the done thing to be a law-breaker, and fear rules. I managed to isolate the core, and those who had been under their influence found it much wiser to be at peace with me than continue as they had been doing.

When I went from the Mount School to the High School three years later God almost immediately took away the special mantle that had been with me. The High School did not need that kind of discipline. I found that it had been with me for a season for God's purposes. I will never forget that prowling evil beast that stalked the corridors, and God met it through me face to face and crushed it and broke it. It was broken at the centre, and there was no difficulty at the perimeter. The pupils learned to do what they were told immediately. I could have an assembly, hundreds strong; in the Mount it would be about six hundred. When I spoke, as the saying goes, 'no dog was allowed to bark'. I mean it. They needed discipline, and I would just have said to anyone who dared to speak, 'Right, Kenneth, my door!' and a

profound silence would fall across the whole company –
and certainly across Kenneth.

An Unsavoury Interlude

I won't go into all the sordid details – the details of the
disciplinary process. Some of it was quite funny. One
rascal who had been absent when the purge fell came back
(he had been truanting, you see, and he knew not that a
new Pharaoh had risen in the land). And I think he had
either been swearing at a teacher or filling his mouth with
water and slushing it all around him. (I may be confusing
two cases – both of which certainly happened.) Anyway,
he landed in my room. His name was Dobbin, and I said,
'Well, Dobbin, I'm going to whack you.' (Those were the
days of corporal punishment.)

'Oh,' he said, 'I'm not takin' it.'

I said, 'I'm not asking you. There's a difference between
getting something and taking something, and you are
about to get something.' He stuck his hands in the pockets
of his jeans, and his jeans were tight. So I whacked him on
one buttock, and while he jumped I whacked him on the
other.

'Oh,' he says, 'you cannae dae this tae me, ye cannae
dae this.'

'Oh, but I'm daein' it.'

I then caught him and put one hand up his back and
delivered half-strokes. I said, 'Now, Dobbin, this isn't
your punishment, you realize. I'm only softening you up.
This isn't your real punishment.'

'Oh,' he says, 'Ah've hud it, Ah've hud it.'

I said, 'No, you huvenae hud it at a'. Now just you get
up and take your punishment like a man.' So up he got.
But this business of taking it like a man didn't appeal to
him at all, so he jumped round behind my desk. And it was
hi-di-di-diddle around that desk – which was not quite in
keeping with the dignity of the headmaster. Meantime the
conversation between us was interesting. He shouted to

me, 'Ah waant a transfer oot o' here.' 'Transfer?' I said. 'I'll transfix you! The only transfer you'll get will be to an approved school.'

'That', he said, 'would be better'n this!'

To bring matters to a conclusion I thought, 'I'll go right round the desk after him, and although he'll run for the door I'll be able to catch him before he gets out.' But don't you believe it: he was out of the door like greased lightning. He evaded my deputy head, who was waiting outside, and sped to a flight of stairs leading out of the building. He tripped at the top and went down the lot on his back. My deputy, pursuing him, did the same.

So there they were lying, the boy with his head on the bottom step. And he was moaning, 'Aw, ma back, ma back!'

While things looked bad, I had a peculiar sense that there was nothing much wrong, so like the Mikado with my black gown around me I made my dignified way to the top of the steps and said in a sepulchral voice, 'Well, Dobbin, it doesn't pay to run away from the headmaster, does it?'

'Aw, ma back, ma back!'

I said, 'Up you come,' and I took him in and doctored him up a bit and sent him home.

I knew he was due to go to court if he was absent again, but I thought, 'Because of his fall I'll give him a day or two without letting proceedings start.'

In due time one of my PE teachers came in and said, 'There's a boy called Dobbin in one of my classes. I hardly know him because he's been absent so much, but he's wanting to get off PE because there's something wrong with his back, and he says you know about it.'

'Oh,' I said, 'yes, so I do, indeed I do. Tell Dobbin I am very worried about that back of his and we'll need to strengthen it. Tell him that every time he comes into the gym, you are to hang him from the second top wall bar (and the boys will know what that means) with knees up!

And he has to touch his toes a hundred times!' (Of course, I was joking.)

Dobbin and I became good friends – as most of my thugs and rascals ultimately did. But the power of the opposition had to be broken. I could entertain you, or maybe shock you, for hours with stories of what happened in its breaking. I had to deal with an evil spiritual power at the centre of the opposition.

Encounters Worldwide

I now want to bring you a number of extracts which highlight realms of spiritual conflict about which most Christians know little and which, in my view, are of vital importance. The selections, which range over various parts of the world, come from a very illuminating collection of essays edited by C. Peter Wagner under the title of *Territorial Spirits: Insights on Strategic-Level Spiritual Warfare from Nineteen Christian Leaders.*[3]

The first extract, from an essay by John Dawson of Youth with a Mission, describes how an evangelistic breakthrough in a city of Argentina did not come until the ruling spirit of the city had been discerned and countered.

> Cordoba, Argentina, is a city of proud and fashion conscious people. Position, possessions, and appearance are of prime importance to 1.1 million living here, who are largely of German and Italian descent.
>
> The Youth With a Mission team I led to Cordoba was made up of Christians from more than 20 nations. We were dressed simply, struggling with Spanish and carrying gospel literature. We really felt like nerds.
>
> The crowds were there. Thousands of Argentines from all over the country had come to see the world soccer playoffs. But our witnessing seemed to lack power. No one was coming to know Christ. The

next day, all 200 of us met for prayer in a rented monastery on the edge of town. We cried out to God for answer.

During that day of prayer and fasting, the Holy Spirit began to reveal the nature of the unseen realm over Cordoba. We realized that our timidity and weakness in proclaiming the gospel was partly due to satanic forces at work in the culture. We discerned a principality attempting to rule the city with 'pride of life.' The only way to overcome a spirit of pride is with the humility of Jesus. So, with the Holy Spirit guiding, we decided to come against the principality in the opposite spirit.

The next day our entire group went downtown. We formed smaller teams of about 30 and walked into the open-air malls. We knelt down right there in the midst of the fashion parade, surrounded by expensive bistros, sidewalk cafes, and boutiques. With our foreheads to the cobblestones, we prayed for a revelation of Jesus to come to the city.

Breakthrough was immediate – breakthrough in us and breakthrough in the city. Large crowds of curious people began to gather around each group.

I vividly remember how Christ strengthened me when I set aside my dignity and knelt in the street. The intimidation of the enemy was broken along with our own pride. As the crowd became larger, I stood to my feet and began to explain through an interpreter why we had come to the city. As I lifted my voice to communicate to the people at the edge of the crowd, the boldness and compassion of the Lord filled me.

All over downtown Cordoba that day, team members preached to attentive audiences. We reaped a harvest of souls. The people were receptive to the point of insisting that we autograph the gospel tracts we gave them! This warm response continued for several weeks until our departure.

Now tell me: how could a city so resistant to the gospel suddenly become a place of harvest? Satan holds the cities and nations by accusation and deception. These are his only weapons. When we minister in a city, we are hindered by that which is deceiving the people. In Cordoba, we were hindered by the spirit of pride that filled the city.

How do we overcome the enemy? We discern the nature of his deception and come in the opposite spirit. Being careful to resist temptation ourselves, we continue in united prayer until authority is gained and God breaks through.[4]

The strategic elements in territorial warfare are explored by the American journalist Steven Lawson in an essay which draws on a number of authorities. On the nature and organization of demons he writes:

Wagner tells of Friday Thomas Ajah – a Sunday school superintendent at the Assemblies of God church in Oribe, Port Harcourt, Nigeria – who was a high-ranking occult leader before his conversion. Ajah was purportedly given the name of St. Thomas the Divine by Satan. He reports that Satan had assigned him control of 12 spirits and that each spirit controlled 600 demons for a total of 7,212.

'I was in touch with all the spirits controlling each town in Nigeria, and I had a shrine in all the major cities,' Ajah says.

The nature of demons can be argued. Some theologians such as Wagner contend that these spirits can attach themselves to people, buildings, seats of government and other objects. Others offer a more vague description, contending that since demons also battle in the heavenlies they have attributes humans cannot comprehend just as angels cannot be fully understood.[5]

On the means by which demonic forces gain entry to a particular region, Lawson writes:

> [John] Dawson differentiates between 'points of entry' and 'dominant features' of a region. A point of entry would be a historic event, such as the slave trade, that gave sin a place in the community, thus enabling demonic forces to establish a foothold. According to Dawson, geographical areas have dominant features that can either be used to glorify God or to advance Satan and sinful activity and obstruct the gospel from being spread.
>
> He uses his own city of Los Angeles as an example, saying that communication is the dominant feature there. As proof, he offers evidence that Southern California is one of the world's largest centers of pornography distribution and the home of the film and television industry, which has sent messages propagating sinful lifestyles around the world. On the other hand, Los Angeles is also home to some major Christian ministries . . . [6]

Lawson draws attention to particular problems of confronting territorial (as opposed to lesser) spirits:

> The New Testament makes it clear that Jesus and His disciples dealt with demons. On one occasion, Jesus cast a legion of demons into a herd of swine (Mark 5:1–15). He also charged His disciples to cast out demons (Matthew 10:7–8), and the book of Acts records their confrontations with evil spirits. Their ministry is used as an example to indicate that we should be doing the same today.
>
> But when it comes to dealing with territorial principalities, it is not quite so clear what we should be doing. C. Peter Wagner says one of the many questions regarding territorial spirits is whether or not Christians can confront them directly.

'It can be very dangerous,' says Wagner. 'There are horror stories where people's ministries were wiped out when they tried this.'

In West Africa, Wagner says, a pastor flippantly ordered a tree cut down that had long been called 'the devil's tree' and identified with a local witch doctor. The second the tree was felled, the pastor dropped dead. Was it demons? Wagner sees a possible connection . . . [7]

The question is thus raised of the Christian's strategy in approaching territorial spirits. The story of Cordoba (above) suggests part of the answer. Writing further on Argentina, Wagner illustrates the importance of prayer and fasting:

Among my personal circle of friends, the one who has had the most experience in dealing with territorial spirits is Argentine Omar Cabrera, pastor of the Vision of the Future Church. A unique feature of his church is that it is decentralized, meeting in 40 or more cities simultaneously throughout the central region of Argentina. Omar and his wife, Marfa, travel 7,000 miles a month, mostly by automobile, leading the church, which numbers some 90,000. How does he move into a new location for his church?

His general practice, after the potential site is selected, is to check into a hotel and seclude himself alone in a room in prayer and fasting. It usually takes the first two or three days to allow the Holy Spirit to cleanse him, to help him disassociate himself, and to identify with Jesus. He feels he 'leaves the world' and is in another realm where the spiritual warfare takes place. The attacks of the enemy at times become fierce. He has even seen some spirits in physical form. His objective is to learn their names and break their power over the city. It usually takes five to eight days, but sometimes more. Once he spent 45 days in conflict. But when he finishes, people in his meetings frequently are saved and healed even before he preaches or prays for them.

I have previously described the tremendous growth of churches in Argentina today and the power evangelism that is accompanying it. I have talked for hours with friends like Omar Cabrera and Edgardo Silvoso listening to them analyze what seems to be behind the extraordinary moving of God in that nation since the Falkland Islands war of 1982.[8]

To the evidence from Argentina Wagner adds confirmation from many other sources that the power of territorial spirits can be broken.

Timothy Warner of Trinity Evangelical Divinity School believes that pioneer missionaries especially need to be prepared to break the power of spirits that rule territories. He relates incidents from missionaries to Indians in Canada and Papua New Guinea where this was actually done.[9]

Paul Yonggi Cho describes an interview with an American Presbyterian chaplain who had experienced a dry, fruitless ministry among the military in Germany, but in Korea 'suddenly heaven opens and the Spirit pours out.' Cho says that in Germany 'the powers of the sky were not broken because the German church did not pray.' In Korea the 'atmosphere of the air' is different, because the cosmic evil powers have been broken. In Korea, Cho says, 'There is not so much pollution as we are a praying church.' He cites the early morning prayer meetings, the all-night prayer meetings and the prayer mountains that are all very much a part of Korean church life.[10]

The same principle is illustrated from Thailand:

> Bill Jackson tells in *World Christian* magazine of a missionary couple in Thailand, who saw no fruit for years until they decided to set one day a week aside to go into the woods and engage the territorial spirits in warfare. A wave of conversions followed. Jackson believes that thousands of unreached peoples are currently under the direct thumb of Satan, and 'The gospel won't go forward among these peoples until we bind the spirits that bind them, whether those deceptive forces be Islam, Hinduism, or any of a myriad of others.'[11]

The contrast between an area in which the satanic grip has been broken and that in which it still reigns is vividly suggested by the example of a town straddling the Brazil-Uruguay border:

> In recent years churches have been growing rapidly in Brazil, but very slowly in neighboring Uruguay. A missionary who met Ralph Mahoney of World MAP had a strange experience while distributing tracts in a small town on the border of Brazil and Uruguay, where the main street divided the two nations. He found that on the Uruguay side no one would accept the tracts, while they received them gratefully on the Brazilian side of the street. And individuals who refused them on the Uruguay side would change their attitude and take them on the Brazilian side. The missionary's interpretation was that 'in crossing the street they were passing out from under the covering of darkness in Uruguay into a country that had experienced, in part, the removing of the covering.'[12]

An essay by an American pastor brings confirmation of Wagner's thesis nearer home. Larry Lea describes in graphic detail how the power of the strong man was bound in Rockwall, Texas:

As the Church on the Rock grew in numbers, the Lord revealed to me in my times of prayer that my primary job as a pastor was to break through the spiritual darkness over Rockwall and over the lives of those He wanted to bring into our congregation. I knew beyond any shadow of a doubt that great preaching wouldn't cause souls to be saved and the church to grow. Finely honed theology spelled out in precise statements wouldn't do it. No, only the tearing down of strongholds that were holding back the people from experiencing God in their lives would cause the church to grow.

So I went to the church building on Saturday nights to pray especially for the services the next day. Often I met others there, but on one particular Saturday night I was alone. The church auditorium was dark, with only one light on above the baptistry in front.

As I knelt there and cried aloud to the Lord, I broke through into a spiritual dimension that I don't know how to describe for you. I was in 'rarified air' (sic) spiritually speaking. When I declared to the North, South, East and West to give up what belongs to the Church on the Rock, I felt a presence in that auditorium that was unlike anything I had ever experienced. And it was **not** a holy presence.

I was kneeling with my eyes closed, and at that moment when I felt this presence in the room, I looked up and in my spiritual vision I saw a being standing in front of me. He was holding a large silver chain in his hands. I'll never forget it as long as I live.

My first impulse was to get up and run out of the building. But at the same time, I knew that I was at a moment of truth, a divine intersection. I realized that I was face-to-face with the very power that was holding back the harvest of souls that God wanted to bring into the Church on the Rock.

The being communicated to me these words, 'Do you really mean it? Are you serious? Are you really going to take your stand?'

Immediately that inner Man within me – the One the Scriptures refer to as 'greater . . . than he that is in the world' – stood up. Before I knew what I was doing, I literally stood to my feet and shouted back at this being, 'You're mighty right I mean what I'm saying!'

I stepped toward him, and when I did, he stepped back. I knew I had him on the run. He dropped the chain and disappeared. He was gone.

From that day to this, I have never encountered anything like that again. But in the next twelve months, we saw some thirty-four hundred people walk the aisles of the Church on the Rock getting saved or united with our church. We held no special revivals. We conducted no house-to-house canvasses. We sponsored no special membership drives. It happened solely by the power of God shining through the powers of darkness. The strongman had been bound and the kingdom of God released.

Something new is emerging in the spirit realm today. God is calling His church to rise up and become militant warriors who will stand and say to principalities and powers, 'Yes, we are taking a stand. Yes, we mean it. Yes, we declare to you that you will not have our children; you will not have our families; you will not have our churches; you will not have our blessings.' And we will drive back the darkness so that the glory of God might shine more strongly.

God's desire is for you to pray this way. Believe it!

What's the purpose of prayer anyway? Prayer is not coming to God to convince Him to do something He doesn't want to do. Prayer is coming into agreement with God about something He already wants to do. It's saying, 'I'll do my part so that You, Lord, are free to do Your part.'[13]

Larry Lea concludes:

We are to stand strong in the honor, love and courage of God and cry out, 'Give up, enemies to the North, everything God has for me, for my family, for my church. Give up, enemies of the South, everything God has for me, for my family, for my church. Give up, enemies of the East, everything God has for me, for my family, and for my church. Give up, enemies of the West, everything God has for me, for my family and for my church. Give it up! It's mine! It's ours!

God says, 'I'll do it. If you'll speak to the enemy like that, I'll do My part. I'll cause things to come your way. It will happen.'

When you declare these things, believe that they are done on earth as they are in heaven. When you start to fight battles like that, winning them for the Lord, though the world situation gets darker and darker, you'll shine brighter and brighter. As those in the world feel worse and worse, you'll be feeling better and better. As the world's systems get weaker and weaker, you'll grow stronger and stronger. As the world starts winding down, you'll be winding up. Instead of wondering what will happen next, you'll be asking, 'Where's the next victory, Lord?'

Give God the glory, for the great works He has done, is doing and will do. The victory is ours. It's yours. It's mine. It's a sure victory if we'll but fight the fight.[14]

The assured victory is based on Christ's work on the cross, as Michael Green emphasizes in an essay that puts the whole subject of spiritual warfare into its theological context. In a section summarizing Scots professor James Stewart's teaching on the relation between cosmic battle and Calvary, he writes:

> These principalities and powers which thwart his will are not independent military units opposing his own army. They are rebel forces of his own. In Christ they were created (Colossians 1:16) and in Christ they were defeated (Colossians 2:15). Philippians 2:10 makes it quite plain that they must own his sway whether they like it or not. His lordship, since the resurrection, has been beyond cavil among beings celestial, terrestrial and subterranean. 'In the end,' writes Stewart, 'the same invisible powers are the tribute which the Son hands over to the Father, that "God may be all in all."' He concludes this short but important article by pointing out that our real battle is not 'with Communism or Caesarism but with the invisible realm where sinister forces stand flaming and fanatic against the rule of Christ. And the only way to meet that demonic mystic passion is with the passion of the Lord.'
>
> There is little doubt that Stewart has stressed a critical aspect in the cross of Christ ... The power of Satan was shattered on that cross, shattered by the invincible power of love.[15]

Triumph of the Cross

And I want to speak to you directly in closing. You say, where do you focus attention? Where and on what do you want us to think as we come to a close of this study? There is one wonderful verse about the cross of Jesus. Paul in wonderfully descriptive and allusive language speaks of that cross where Christ triumphed over the powers of darkness and made a show of them openly. Those of you who are students may know that this picture is taken from something which happened regularly in ancient Rome.

A Roman general returning to Rome after having been away at war had to stop at the River Rubicon and leave his army there. If he crossed the Rubicon with his soldiers he would be regarded as a traitor in rebellion, and the Senate would take action against him. But from time to time the Senate granted a triumphal entry to a victorious general. That meant that he came back into Rome with all his army.

I want you to picture what lies behind that scriptural reference. There sat Rome, the city on the seven hills. The first half of the army went into the city, rank upon rank, to the welcome, the huzzahs, the bunting: high holiday in Rome. And there in the middle of the army came the victorious general, drawn in a chariot by milk-white horses, standing erect; chained to his chariot wheels were the great men, the generals that he had fought against and taken captive, the kings and princes, even a queen such as Boadicea. They were chained to the chariot wheels as the pennants and the standards and the flags were held aloft, and they were made a show of openly. The cavalcade surged into the city, and the second part of the army came in behind. The cries arose: *Hail Caesar! Vive imperator!*

And the picture Paul is giving: into the eternal, the heavenly Jerusalem, the Old Testament saints go rank upon rank upon rank. There in the midst comes the Lord Jesus, and His cross is transformed into a triumphal chariot. There he stands erect in the day of His glory. And there chained to the 'chariot wheels' of His cross are the principalities and the powers and the rulers of darkness, the strong man and all His emissaries – chained to the chariot wheels of Jesus. And there behind them, rank upon rank, comes the New Testament church. And we are not shouting, *Vive imperator*, but *Unto Him that loved us and washed us in His own blood, to Him be the power and the glory for ever, Amen.* Can you feel the joy of it rise in your soul – the victory of Jesus? And what about these principalities and powers? They are broken. Their power is broken. They are in chains.

I want to direct you to the cross. I want you to see the cross of Jesus outside the city wall, and the principalities and powers that were behind both the cruelty of the Roman Empire and the irreligion of the religious Jews, the evil spirits that were having effect on Jew and on Gentile. I want you to see the controversy of the ages between God and Satan centring on that cross, and the dark powers coming from all over the world. And from the sixth to the ninth hour there is darkness over all the land, there is surging, surging darkness: **This is your hour and the power of darkness**. Oh, the cross is wonderful. The picture is wonderful. You feel that Satan has hounded Christ to the cross. And yet in a sense he didn't, you know. The initiative was not in his hands. Ah, no, there is a deeper picture beneath the surface. Where is God in the matter? What is the action of God? In the ministry of deliverance there is a parallel. We don't always have to wait until **the demon is pleased** to come up for a fight. **The power of Christ compels the demon** to the surface. And Christ took the initiative. He came for the very purpose of going to the cross. Mark that. He deliberately went to the cross. Did you think Satan drove Him there? I tell you, it is as though He had Satan by the throat, and He dragged him to Calvary. Yes! Satan was compelled to come out with all his foul forces, and he came out at the cross to receive the death wound from which there is no recovery through all eternity. Did you think Christ was defeated on the cross? He was never defeated.

> By meekness and defeat
> He won the meed and crown,
> Trod all His foes beneath His feet
> By being trodden down.

I'm proud of the Christ of the cross! I often say that were I an artist I would love to paint this picture: I'd love to paint the picture of that swift-flowing river of death and show Jesus going down under the waters a conqueror. I would have a glorious light shining on His upturned face. He died a victor; He didn't die defeated.

Fruits of Victory

And have you ever thought of the glory of the next episode? I think that Satan possibly even up to that point thought he was victor. And I believe that Satan was there at the gates of Hades, where he had imprisoned every soul of man that had died from Adam to that day. He had them there in upper or in lower Hades, as the case might be. I picture him waiting to put Christ there. I have often wondered whether he or Christ got to the gates first, but oh, I love my picture of that moment of meeting. I see the strong Son of God with one backward blow lay Satan on the ground, and take the keys of the kingdom of death from his girdle, and go into that upper place. Oh, what a wonderful hour! See them there, all those in upper Hades who were destined for eternal glory. They had been held in a kind of bondage, unfree: Jesus comes in. Adam is there: now the last Adam comes. Abraham, Isaac, Jacob, Daniel, Shadrach, Meshach, Abednego, Joshua ... All the Old Testament saints are there: and Jesus comes in. Oh, I can see them, as they bow to the ground before Him. This hour is central in the ages. The victory of the cross begins to be outworked. With power and with glory He takes them with one sweep up through the shattered gates of death to Paradise! – the Conqueror, the Beloved.

Our legal power is in the cross, and we can say to the devil, 'Begone! A stronger than you has bound you and is binding you,' and we enter into the fruit of His triumph. Blessed be the Name of the Lord forever. We are on the road to eternal glory, not damnation. We are on the road to eternal victory, and God wants us to enjoy it **now**. He wants us to reap the fruits of Calvary in our earth life. And we have only got one life.

I stood at my grandmother's open grave. She died in her ninety-third year. I'd be about twenty-five at the time.

And I loved my grandmother, but, you know, I wasn't shedding tears that day. She was an old lady and we expected her to go. I stood at that graveside, and I thought, 'Oh, God! I've only got a short time left. Even if I live to ninety, there is very little time left to do much for You.' I came away from that grave to preach the gospel of Christ. And I have never ceased. He has made provision for effective ministry, and if we appear before Him ineffective people, we'll bear the responsibility and face the judgment. Christ is Lord. Can you not feel Him around you now? Can you not feel the sense of that presence around you?

Shall we pray. Shall we just worship for a moment or two, and let the presence of Christ be with us. Feel His presence. Know His power.

> *Prayer*: Lord, leave now Your blessing, we ask, in Christ's Name and for His sake. Amen.

Notes

[1] For Mary MacLean's story, see Hugh Black, *The Clash of Tongues: With Glimpses of Revival* (New Dawn Books, 1988), Part 2.

[2] The Lewis revivals of 1939 and 1949 are featured in various of my own books, especially *Revival: Personal Encounters*. For Duncan Campbell and the '49 revival, see Andrew A. Woolsey, *Channel of Revival: A Biography of Duncan Campbell* (The Faith Mission, 1974).

[3] Published by Sovereign World, 1991.

[4] John Dawson, 'Seventh Time Around: Breaking Through a City's Invisible Barriers to the Gospel,' originally published in David Bryant, ed., *Prayer Pacesetters Sourcebook* (Concerts of Prayer International, 1989); culled from Wagner, ed., *Territorial Spirits*, pp. 135–7.

[5] Steven Lawson, 'Defeating Territorial Spirits,' originally published in *Charisma & Christian Life* magazine (Strang Communications Company, 1990); culled from Wagner, *Territorial Spirits*, pp. 35–6.

[6] *Ibid.*, p. 37.

[7] *Ibid.*, pp. 38–9.

[8] C. Peter Wagner, 'Territorial Spirits,' originally published in his *How to Have a Healing Ministry without Making Your Church Sick* (Ventura, California: Regal Books, 1988); culled from Wagner, *Territorial Spirits*, pp. 45–6.

[9] Wagner's source is Timothy M. Warner, 'Power Encounter with the Demonic,' in Robert E. Coleman, ed., *Evangelism on the Cutting Edge* (Fleming H. Revell, 1986), pp. 98, 99.

[10] Wagner, 'Territorial Spirits,' in his *Territorial Spirits*, p. 47.

[11] *Ibid.*

[12] *Ibid.*, pp. 47–8.

[13] Larry Lea, 'Binding the Strongman' (in Wagner, *Territorial Spirits*, pp. 83–95), pp. 91–3.

[14] *Ibid.*, pp. 94–5.

[15] Michael Green, 'Principalities and Powers,' originally published in *I Believe in Satan's Downfall* (William B. Eerdmans Publishing Company, 1981); culled from Wagner, *Territorial Spirits*, pp. 187–8. For the material on Stewart, Green cites the *Scottish Journal of Theology*, 1951.

Chapter 6

Encounters with Territorial Spirits

In 1992 we entered a period of unusual development on the material front. God's guidance was to go forward. After the second of two newly acquired buildings was in our hands we were confronted with a very powerful spiritual adversary. The story may seem strange to many in this twentieth century. It is true nevertheless. Let me sketch the background.

Story of a Bookshop

Part way through 1992 we decided to buy land adjoining our church at West Stewart Street, Greenock, for the purpose of erecting a coffee/bookshop to give a point of close contact with the community and provide a much needed Christian literature centre. At first the local authority insisted on extensive car parking, and the ground left for development was much too small to be practical. Thanks to the persistence of our treasurer, Mr Chris Jewell, this was reversed and a larger building without car parking provision was allowed.

The cost of the ground was over £36,000 and the first estimated building costs were in the region of £800,000. I felt a distinct check on my spirit at this prospect, and ultimately revised plans for something nearer £500,000 were submitted. At this point we had about £250,000 available, leaving us to find approximately £250,000 in the course of one year. That is very much in excess of what normally comes in over such a short time (we have no really rich people in our fellowship).

The matter was put to the people and in the first special offering more than £40,000 came in, including two gifts of over £10,000 each. We made arrangements with our bank for a facility of £250,000 should such be required. Building commenced and after a few months our treasurer came to me intimating that this sum would not be needed: £130,000 would do. A few more months passed and he then indicated that £30,000 would do. About two or three months before the opening he reported that no borrowing at all would be required. The money was all in and we opened the New Dawn Bookshop and Connection Coffee House totally free of debt. I would again stress that we have no wealthy people amongst us.

As it happened, about the time we planned to build in Greenock, a church in another area came on the market. This area will be referred to as X-----, for the sake of confidential material in a later episode. The building we were using there had become much too small and we offered £30,000 for the alternative accommodation. Our bid was unsuccessful and we were left in real difficulty.

A Church Provided

Almost to the day when the total sum needed for the Greenock coffee/bookshop was in, I had a letter from a friend who had been anxious for a long time that we should find a much larger building in X-----. Wise woman, she did not merely draw my attention to the possibility that a particular building might be coming on the market, but she supplied me with the name together with the business and home telephone numbers of the person to be contacted if this should actually happen.

The recent history of the church concerned was very interesting. It was a List A building, and it had first belonged to the Free Church and then to the Church of Scotland. The latter had sold it to a private individual who was minded to build an independent congregation. He worked hard and did a great deal to preserve and improve the property. While there had been much to encourage him, there came a point when he was uncertain whether to reopen or not after a summer recess. At a critical juncture I telephoned him. He thought this providential because of the precise nature of the timing, and we met. I should mention that the lady who had phoned me had done so on her own initiative and in fact at that point Mr Duthie had no intention of selling. I told him much of our past history as a movement and of God's dealings with me personally. Mr Duthie felt strongly that God Himself was intervening in the matter.

I indicated in some detail how God had been with us in the opening of our various churches across the country and how He had made financial provision. I went on to describe the spiritual background, in particular my own baptism in the Spirit and how God had spoken to me on the island of Lewis and some of the consequences. Over the years thousands had been saved and thousands baptized in the Spirit. I also mentioned a much later occasion when I was again spoken to very particularly about deliverance and the consequences of this.[1] After the Lewis occasion people received the Spirit in great numbers. Since the later occasion many have been delivered from demon power.

As we talked I felt the presence of the Holy Spirit and I could see my friend was affected. He had already sensed the significance in the timing of our approach, and he indicated now that he felt almost as though God had appointed him as a caretaker and that we should in fact have the building.

I then enquired about the price, which was very substantial and would place us back in a very similar position to that in which we had been one year earlier. The church had cost him a great deal to purchase, and he had subsequently spent a lot on it. Had the figure he mentioned been proposed six months earlier I think I would just have shaken hands and told him it had been nice meeting him but we weren't really in the same league. But the fact is that with the building of the coffee/book-shop and the way architects and builders tossed around figures in the region of £20,000 or £50,000 like confetti (for various small alterations), my attitude to the value of money had really changed. I had got to the stage of think-ing: if you are £100,000 in the red, £120,000 isn't all that different! I was reminded of my old father-in-law who was a very liberal man but who never did come to terms with the altering value of money. Ten shillings was a fortune to him to his dying day. In any case, a miracle had happened in me, and I was also keenly aware of how God had made recent provision. I was prepared to consider Mr Duthie's figure. I felt God telling me not to stagger through unbelief, and I also felt Him give me intimation not to drive a hard bargain.

Now those who know me best and know me as a farmer's son, are very well aware that like the rest of my breed I enjoy a bit of haggling – not really for the money side of it, but for the fun of it. Farmers just love to get a bargain – but I felt not to do this. My friend had done well by the building and that, I imagine, largely out of his own pocket, and he was to be dealt with kindly.[2] To cut a long story short, our offer was accepted. But there remained one possible barrier: there was a legal obligation that in the event of his selling, the Church of Scotland had a right of re-purchase. A personal friend, the Reverend Jack McArthur, who was a member of the Presbytery, happened for the first time to be attending the committee which dealt with such matters, and lo, ours was the first item on the agenda. He was able to speak about us, and there were no objections to the purchase.

We had no doubt that the hand of God was in the matter, and you might imagine that from that point all would be plain sailing. But it was not so, and indeed it is because of what follows that the story is included here. The financial side was secure, but the spiritual war commenced.

Ominous Signs

When a small group of our people first went in to inspect the building, one young lady indicated to me that there was something wrong, and particularly in one part of the building. I think she felt 'spooky', if this is the right way to describe her reaction. She said, 'I wouldn't like to spend the night here alone, and I have never felt this in any of our other buildings.' Another of our folks had worked in a nearby house which she maintained was very badly haunted. She said that the lane beside the church was also reputed to be haunted. Rumours of other hauntings, poltergeist activity, ghostly appearances and ghostly assaults in various parts of the area had been quite horrendous and should be viewed as a background to what later emerged.

I was much concerned that no rumour of this should get abroad amongst the congregation and took the two ladies to the lane, where we prayed, and I more or less bound them to silence.

Meanwhile my daughter Mary (the appointed minister of the church), who had felt very happy about the proposed purchase, was taken aback when she encountered the atmosphere outside the building. She felt a fearful coldness in the surrounding area. Deeply concerned, she called for Grace and Diana to come and spiritually inspect matters. Meantime she deliberately said not a word to me in case I should in any way broadcast the matter. There was I, determinedly keeping things from her – and she was doing precisely the same with me!

The Cleansing of the Church

Grace and Diana duly came to the church, and I leave them to tell their own stories, beginning with Diana's:

About fifteen years ago, God gave me a vision of Miss Mary Black standing in the midst of a large church in X-----, ministering to a group of fiery young people. This vision was shared with Mr Black. Indeed, I took him there with Jennifer Offord, and he and I looked in one of the windows. I think the building was on the market at the time.[3]

Last year that same building became available to our church, and we were able to purchase it. It is indeed a lovely building.

At Mary's request I went to visit it one day with Grace, who showed me round every nook and cranny. It took us an hour, such is the size of the building.

After going round it Grace told me that Mary wanted us to pray over the building. 'Were there any parts that I was uncomfortable in? Did I want to go round the whole building again to see?' I decided that I could remember the parts where I sensed a coldness, and Grace was in agreement with my feelings. The building was not haunted, but perhaps had not been as full of the presence of God as it should have been, and therefore was more open to the darkness in the surrounding area without the church.

We went to a certain part and began to pray. It was a hard fight against the darkness. We were aware of a lot of demonic activity outside the building, of ruling spirits over the area, dominating the atmosphere without and within the church. It seemed as though one strong demonic presence sat dominating and covering the very building.

As we prayed Christ came. Gradually, oh, so gradually, the atmosphere began to change until one sensed He was in control. I saw in vision Christ walking through the church from the back left-hand door right down to the front. As He moved He left behind Him Light, like waves of light in every pew. The whole church began to fill with that Light until every corner was full. Within the Light there was music. It was not separate from the Light but part of it, and it too filled the whole church.[4]

We saw the angels come, and where one mighty evil spirit had ruled and dominated, now a high angel came and took its place. He stood over the building triumphant. Soon the whole building was completely surrounded by light.

It felt to us now that the church was completely clear of darkness and clothed with light, and we were satisfied with at least that part of the work.

We were both aware that the area outside the building was not clear; we drove round it but did not feel anointing to push beyond what Christ had done that day. I was conscious, however, of a strong sense of darkness in one particular part of a certain street, coming from, I reckoned, three houses. I later learned that it was believed in the locality that three houses in that very part of the street were haunted.

This is how Grace describes the cleansing of the church:

The first time I saw the building I felt daunted and not only by its size, but daunted inwardly, spiritually. The second time I was with my husband Wesley, and as we passed it in the car I felt chilled and repelled, particularly as I looked at the front and the adjoining lane. I arranged to go with Diana to pray in and for the building on Wednesday 9 December. At our Tuesday night prayer meeting in Greenock I expected a good meeting, but I found a dark barrier, connected, I suspect, with our proposed visit. In spirit I saw the outline of the church and a huge dark figure standing in the side lane towering over the roof of the church. I went with Diana next morning and we both agreed to go first to the church flat (one of the worst places). I felt some parts of the church, such as the flat, were shadowed rather than having a demon resident in them.

We prayed in the kitchen of the flat and I felt a tremendous power (indeed, a new depth of power). We prayed until I seemed to see a great angelic figure fight the dark one and displace him. I saw the fight on the roof, and I saw the angel's wings overspreading the roof. Then light poured over the roof and a wonderful presence of Christ filled the flat. This all happened while we were still in the flat. We then went downstairs and walked through the lesser halls and felt them fill up with the presence of Christ. We continued to the vestry and discussed what we had each felt.

We had both felt the angelic presence (before we talked to each other). We had both been reminded of the prince of the power of Persia (Daniel 10:13, 20). We prayed in the vestry and I found my spirit probing around the park area outside, and I felt there was a rustling amongst the lesser demons. I then felt that a band of protection came right around the wall of the church, though an angel stood with a flaming sword outside the front entrance door guarding it.

As we drove away I saw that the church was totally different. The chill was gone. There was the feeling of a dawning light and a warmth. In the flat there had been prayer for an impact on the area. As we drove around the gardens and streets we were aware that the feeling was not good and there was still much to be done. We left, however, with a wonderful sense of the presence of God, with joy and exultation in Christ, and deeply moved that He trusted our church, trusted us with the power of His presence. He had committed Himself to us. We both felt we broke new ground in the experiences of that day.

Very soon after the events described above I took notes from both Diana and Grace and include some additional points not specifically mentioned in their accounts.

Some time after the experience both ladies felt revival coming nearer – a sense of the power of revival. There was a clear sense too of territorial spirit warfare.

Both felt a protecting band coming round the church. Diana felt light pouring out from within to break the power of darkness in the lane.

Diana saw the blood of Christ come right down to the ground in front of the building for its protection.

Initially Diana had been unhappy with the atmosphere in the flat, at the front of the building and in both the side and back lanes. There was a darkness covering the building and possibly controlling the area around, and while there was no demon inside the building it was as though darkness was seeping in. Diana felt the presence of Christ had claimed the building. Christ walked through the church and she saw His garments as folds of light; the folds were left behind from the back to the front as He passed through. An angel like a prince replaced the evil power over the church.

From the vestry both ladies went out in spirit to the lanes and saw light from within shattering the darkness. Both went in spirit to the front at the same time and while Diana felt the blood coming down and was given the words, 'This is holy ground,' Grace sensed the angel at the front door. Both perceived a band of light come down and surround the whole church. On going outside not only Grace but Diana too almost thought that the building looked different.

When Mary next came to the church she sensed a great change, and one of her assistants who had formerly felt like an intruder in the building suddenly felt at home.

And Related Areas

Not all the members of this church were local.

The following incident arose in another area to which I will refer as 'Y-----', not geographically connected to X-----, but closely related in the spiritual world. One way of putting this might be to say that there was a spiritual intersection in the lives of those Christians who had ties with both areas. Again, Grace and Diana were particularly used in this related instance of territorial warfare. Here is Diana's account.

One night in chatting to Mr Black after a very satisfying time of ministry with a girl who had been delivered from an occult spirit, he mentioned to Grace and me that there was another 'haunted house' case coming up.

The house this time had recently been purchased by very spiritual people, one of whom was deeply involved in the work in X----- (although the house was in another locality). She had been locking up late one night, and was left with the distinct impression that there was someone behind her performing almost the same action. She had turned to look behind her, to see the figure of a man. There were other signs in the house that all was not well, and other members of the household began to be disturbed also.

When we arrived at the house we were taken to the spot where 'the man' had been seen, and a group of us began to pray. It seemed to me as though nothing stirred. Grace and I then asked to be alone, and we sought for that wonderful anointing that comes from above and breaks any power of darkness in an instant.

As we entered more deeply into the place of prayer we met with an evil power that was extremely stubborn and reluctant to go. Without any words it seemed to communicate to us that it was not prepared to move, and that it had every right and intention of staying. As the presence of Christ intensified, the darkness was broken and the entity was cast out of the house.

Over several weeks at the beginning of this year I had felt very strained spiritually for no apparent reason. I could not put my finger on the trouble, but there just didn't seem to be a break from the constant pressure inside. A verse that helped immensely during this time was

> *Rejoice not over me, O my enemy;*
> *When I fall, I shall rise;*
> *When I sit in darkness,*
> *The LORD will be a light to me.*   (Micah 7:8 RSV)

Around that time I was chatting to Grace, to discover that she too was under similar assault. She spoke of the darkness over the area of the church in X----- and the assault Mary was experiencing as she broke new ground there. Suddenly I saw the connection; that in itself was quite a relief!

Grace and I both felt drawn to fast – something that I have found extremely useful against the powers of darkness. I find spiritually things become sharper, and I operate on a higher dimension. Through prayer I felt as though a wall of blackness that I had been facing for weeks began to crack. Again and again as I prayed I felt more and more ground taken in the locality until the particular part which had been so dark was clear. In prayer victory came.

Grace and I then went to the area around the church, and we started at the spot which had seemed so dark. Together we prayed, and to my surprise we could sense nothing. It was wonderful to see the effectiveness of prayer miles from the locality. So we drove round the area in the car, and as we drove we both sensed immediately a terrible darkness coming from another part. This was not the same evil power that I had met in prayer; this was another.

We prayed and, oh, what a wonderful anointing came. The dark power just crumbled before Him; it could not stand His wonderful presence; and we knew that victory had come over a far wider area.

It was very satisfying to hear from Mary in the following week that she too felt a considerable change, starting from that night. But there was more yet to come.

As powers of righteousness and angelic beings communicate, so do powers of darkness.

Although there had been a considerable improvement for Mary in the new building, there was not the complete change that she was looking for. So we opened ourselves to prayer and fasting again. This time we found that demonic powers over the neighbourhood of the house in Y----- for which we had earlier prayed were preventing the complete breakthrough in the work in X-----. It was not altogether incomprehensible that such a thing should happen. People had been coming from Y----- to support the meetings – some of whom had had connections with the recently cleansed house. In fact we felt that the darkness we had met within that house had only been part of a ruling darkness that was surrounding the house and area outside.

It was very similar to the first occasion when we had prayed around the church at X-----. We spent much time alone and in prayer before the occasion and felt a considerable breakthrough. I can foresee a time when we will not need to go to areas concerned 'but only say the word, Lord,' and it shall be done (cf. Matthew 8:8).

Grace and I met one Thursday evening and drove around the locality of the house, stopping at two different places to pray. At the first place there was a significant breakthrough, and at the second victory was complete. It was like something tall and strong being broken up and falling to the ground as nothing, and then He came. It is worth all the struggle just for those precious moments when we see Him. He is absolutely beautiful! There is no struggle in Him, nor is there any sense that He has had to fight something horrifically dark – one word of His power and it is done. I had a sense of Christ walking along the streets where the darkness had been, and where there had been that ominous presence there was now peace, quietness and light.

The rest of the story is lovely. Mary, who had battled with the powers of darkness for months, felt a complete change, and the awful darkness she had been facing as she ministered was swept away by His wonderful presence.

Grace's version of the same sequence of events is as follows:

On this occasion it became evident that a house recently bought by godly people in Y----- was haunted. One girl found herself unable to read or pray in her room; another found herself conscious of a definite presence beside her. These things could be described in more detail, but I never like dwelling on the dark side or giving too much attention to Satan.

Again I encountered the presence in the spiritual world before going to the house. We prayed where we felt the presence particularly bad and it was forced to retreat before the presence of Christ. We did not feel the house was clear, but with one accord went to the room mentioned above. We prayed here for quite a long time, but ultimately knew the expelling of darkness before the incoming light of God. I probed in my spirit to see if we should go to other rooms, particularly one which I had not been too happy about, but I saw light streaming from that room out through the window. Praise His Name. The people in the house felt a tremendous difference. The girl in whose room we had prayed came home and, without hearing from us the outcome of our visit, felt a complete change in the atmosphere as soon as she entered the bedroom.

These things are very real, but there is absolutely no fear in dealing with them when under anointing, so great and certain is the power of the Lord Jesus Christ. Diana prayed that any presence left would come with us, not stay in the house! It lingered around us for the next day or two, but about two mornings after the visit I suddenly felt it was chained in the pit.

The area around the church in X----- was still to be dealt with. After the occasion of praying in the church there was a significant change, but those ministering there continued to find a terrible darkness, not in the church, but in the area. Though rarely in X----- myself, I kept encountering this darkness during meetings in Y----- and knew it was related to X-----. I suggested to Diana that we go back and pray in one particular part which my spirit had probed on the previous occasion and where I had felt dark minions disturbed by what had happened as Christ cleansed the church. We decided to fast in preparation and ultimately prayed one Sunday night. We parked the car in the spot which we felt was the worst and met unmistakably dark power. It fled, and even the house we had parked outside seemed to look different afterwards. I don't mean to imply that any darkness in houses in the area was all driven out, but the binding power in that part was broken. Mary sensed a tremendous change in the spiritual world.

I felt the work was not quite completed until a week or so later, when Diana and I prayed in a particular part of the other locality referred to earlier. We were conscious that something needed to be broken around the house where we had previously prayed. Again we fasted and met one evening in that area. We prayed until we felt light over a considerable part, especially around and emanating from the house, but we were aware that the real source of darkness was still unbroken. We moved the car and started to pray again. The dark power seemed so strong and flaunting and immovable, but suddenly Christ was there and, so fast that I hardly knew what had happened, I felt as though angelic presences were driving the darkness far away. The presence of Christ was utterly wonderful. I felt Him particularly close then and knew His domination of that area and His desire for it, and sensed a little of what it must be like when revival comes and a whole community, including its very streets, is saturated with the presence of God. I felt Him very close. At first individually and then as a couple we became aware that He really was with us in what we were doing and wanted us to be open to this kind of ministry. The people in the house in that area had a wonderful meeting. They surely must have had; the presence of Christ in the very street was so tangible. The next night I was present at a meeting in X----- and felt that same wonderful presence of His glory, and I think about a week later on the Sunday night Mary had the best meeting she had had in the new church and felt really free of the dark barrier.

It came to my knowledge that another lady had carried an unusual burden in connection with the foregoing matters. She was not aware of the main events which are now recorded. As I learned details of her experience I was reminded of something I had learned long ago: there are often many links in a chain of events leading to a spiritual fulfilment, and we can be gravely mistaken if we think that we alone – either an individual or a small group – are exclusively responsible for a particular spiritual outcome. This lady reports as follows:

During a Tuesday evening prayer meeting I saw in the Spirit a terrible and evil beast crouched as if preparing to pounce and devour. In that same instant I knew that Christ at the critical moment would intervene.

Over the days following I felt the evil eyes trying to draw my spirit towards them, somehow trying to dominate me. I was also on edge, waiting for some event that would be the outworking of the beast pouncing, as I knew that the beast must pounce prior to Christ's intervening.

It was during the Tuesday prayer meeting before the Aberfoyle conference[5] that Grace mentioned the benefits of fasting. On waking that Thursday morning the phrase *This cometh not out but by prayer and fasting* (cf. Matthew 17:21 AV), was in my mind. Hence I fasted that day and experienced a tremendous assurance that the light of Christ was immovable.

At some point during the Aberfoyle conference I saw in the Spirit the Lion of the Tribe of Judah take up position ready to spring. It was strange, because I was like an onlooker waiting for the moment of confrontation between the beast and the Lion but had no clear understanding of what it all meant.

The phrase 'The beast has pounced' came to my mind on the Sunday afternoon. With an absolute certainty I knew that the Lion of the Tribe of Judah had met that beast in mid-spring and destroyed it. Praise His Name!

Notes

[1] For all of these events, see chapter 3 above.

[2] Mr Duthie's side of the story is very interesting. Since he had not made a previous decision to sell, my question regarding price came somewhat out of the blue, and he made a quick mental calculation of what his costs had been. These he hoped to be able to recover but was not out to make money. In the event he revised the figure downward. He wanted God's will in the matter and there was absolutely no haggling between us.

[3] This, I may say, I had totally forgotten – but as I get older there is much I forget – HBB.

[4] It is interesting to hear from others that heavenly singing is frequently heard in the church when no human voices are around. This happened in the case of a couple living in the flat within the church premises. Recently converted, they had no knowledge that such things could happen, as they frequently do in revival time. The first of the family to hear the singing was their married daughter, who on a visit to the flat requested that the door be left open so that she could hear the music. Her mother told her there was no such thing: the congregation had all dispersed. The daughter insisted that she could still hear beautiful singing. One of her parents, wondering if after all there was a choir practice being held in one of the halls, went to investigate – but there was no one in the building. Since then both the father and mother have heard it for themselves. The mother says that she heard it when she was quiet. As soon as she began to analyse it, it would fade, but would return as she ceased to try and understand it.

[5] An annual event, usually held at Aberfoyle.

Chapter 7

Battle to the Gates

A sermon preached by Grace Gault
including reference to events of the preceding chapter

Prayer: We thank Thee for the beauty of Thy presence, we thank Thee for the stillness of it. As in that inner holy of holies the silence and the light engulfed the high priest, so does Thy silence, Thy light, Thy beauty, engulf us as we draw near unto Thee, O living Christ, Thou living bread from heaven, Thou unchanging One, the same yesterday, today and for ever. From eternity to eternity Thou hast been the only begotten of the Father, and Thou art revealed through Thy Spirit, Thou art revealed even to Thy children, Thy redeemed.

> Still, still with Thee, when purple morning
> breaketh,
> When the bird waketh, and the shadows flee

— we waken to Thee. Oh, the joy to waken and find Thee there, the unchanging Christ. And we would that, even as the walls of that temple were clothed with the beauty of the curtains that spoke of Christ, so too may this house, as it fills with the praise of Thy people, become so filled with Thee, O Christ, that the very walls shall seem clothed with the worship, the incense: pure, pure love of Thy redeemed. Take Thy place, Lord. Thou art the very centre of our worship and our life, glorious Christ. Amen.

God spoke to me during the week in one of the clearest words, I think, He has ever given me for a Sunday morning service, and He made it very clear it was for this morning. He also made it clear to me who was to preach tonight (not me)! The word was burning, and I felt it become very opposed, but I found that God was adamant that I should deliver it. The word had been so clear that I knew I just had to preach it. And He has intervened Himself to bring it about.

Shadrach, Meshach and Abednego

The reading is very well known, but it came to me with a new force and in a slightly different way from normal. It concerns the occasion when Nebuchadnezzar had set up the golden image for all his subjects to worship, and Shadrach, Meshach and Abednego refused to obey.

> 'Now when you hear the sound of the horn, flute, zither, lyre, harp, pipes and all kinds of music, if you are ready to fall down and worship the image I made, very good. But if you do not worship it, you will be thrown immediately into a blazing furnace. Then what god will be able to rescue you from my hand?' Shadrach, Meshach and Abednego replied to the king, 'O Nebuchadnezzar, we do not need to defend ourselves before you in this matter. If we are thrown into the blazing furnace, the God we serve is able to save us from it, and he will rescue us from your hand, O king. But even if he does not, we want you to know, O king, that we will not serve your gods or worship the image of gold you have set up. Then Nebuchadnezzar was furious with Shadrach, Meshach and Abednego, and his attitude towards them

changed. He ordered the furnace to be heated seven times hotter than usual and commanded some of the strongest soldiers in his army to tie up Shadrach, Meshach and Abednego and throw them into the blazing furnace. So these men, wearing their robes, trousers, turbans and their other clothes, were bound and thrown into the blazing furnace. The king's command was so urgent and the furnace so hot that the flames of the fire killed the soldiers who took up Shadrach, Meshach and Abednego, and these three men, firmly tied, fell into the blazing furnace. Then king Nebuchadnezzar leapt to his feet in amazement and asked his advisers, 'Weren't there three men we tied up and threw into the fire?' They replied, 'Certainly, O king.' He said, 'Look! I see four men walking around in the fire, unbound and unharmed, and the fourth looks like a son of the gods.' Nebuchadnezzar then approached the opening of the blazing furnace and shouted, 'Shadrach, Meshach and Abednego, servants of the Most High God, come out! Come here!' So Shadrach, Meshach and Abednego came out of the fire, and the satraps, prefects, governors and royal advisers crowded around them. They saw that the fire had not harmed their bodies, nor was a hair of their heads singed; their robes were not scorched, and there was no smell of fire on them. Then Nebuchadnezzar said, 'Praise be to the God of Shadrach, Meshach and Abednego, who has sent his angel and rescued his servants! They trusted in him and defied the king's command and were willing to give up their lives rather than serve or worship any god except their own God. Therefore I decree that the people of any nation or language who say anything against the God of Shadrach, Meshach or Abednego be cut into pieces and their houses be turned into piles of rubble, for no other god can save in this way.' Then the king promoted Shadrach, Meshach and Abednego in the province of Babylon. (Daniel 3:15–30 NIV)

The Strength of the Opposition

Without going into all the background of the story, I want to select certain points. Think of the commandment that Nebuchadnezzar had given and the golden image that was to be worshipped. His commandment was backed by his total authoritative power. We don't know where Daniel was – whether he was exempted because he was so close to the king at this point, or whether he was out of the province – but these three seem to have been alone. And it may be significant that they did not have their leader there.

I want you to see the strength of the opposition that was against them. It wasn't just a casual command: 'You ought to do this, and if not there'll be some trouble.' The golden image (I imagine quite hideous) was set there: 'Worship this: Nebuchadnezzar says so. For a certain space of time you must not worship your God.' The punishment was to be death. These men saw that hellish opposition, and they saw behind the commandment of Nebuchadnezzar. They saw that he was a pawn, I think in some ways just a witless pawn in the hand of the enemy, who was furious at Daniel's success and the honour that had come to God through Daniel's interpretation of Nebuchadnezzar's dream. He was out to destroy: he was having another attempt to destroy the children of Israel and so to destroy Christ – to prevent Christ coming, to destroy you and me, to prevent us ever finding salvation.

And he has come: he has found a tremendous tool, because Nebuchadnezzar has absolute power. God Himself, in the interpretation of the dream, has said of his power and authority that there is no king like Nebuchadnezzar in all the world. He has been allowed that power by God, and he is using it against God! It seems impenetrable, doesn't it, that darkness? It seems absolutely immovable! – that strength of opposition to God, so strong, so powerful. 'And in any case, Shadrach, Meshach and Abednego, if you don't obey, you are going to die, and God will not be worshipped after all, because who else will stand after that?'

I love these three men; I love their fearlessness: 'Our God can deliver us, Nebuchadnezzar. But if not: be it known unto you, we are still not doing this thing. If He doesn't deliver us out of your hand, we are still not worshipping at **your** behest.' They weren't at all apologetic about it. They weren't muttering, 'M'm – hope he doesn't . . . hope he's not too offended. We'll tell him we'll worship God quietly, not openly.' You can sense the utter fearlessness of God in them. 'We're just not doing it. What are you saying? – you are going to heat the furnace seven times? So what? We are still not doing it, Nebuchadnezzar.' And remember, behind Nebuchadnezzar's power, they felt the power of Satan, they felt that hellish opposition; they felt it like an immovable, impenetrable darkness and strength and power, the power of Babylon (I mean, the spiritual power behind Babylon). They were not afraid. They trusted in God that, even if He let them die, He would still deliver them. And Nebuchadnezzar is infuriated by their fearlessness.

I tell you, you who desire to serve Christ, you will come into a battlefield. There are times you will face a hellish opposition that seems immovable, and it is real: it is not in your imagination. It can move through people, it can move through circumstance; it can just be there, quite open and unashamed darkness. The thing you must never do is run away. If you do, it will come after you, and you will be under its heel. The thing you must never do is to allow a flicker of fear. (There is no reason for fear, as you will see in a moment.) Don't be afraid. Stand up to the enemy. It is not you who stands up, but Christ in you. These three men stood against the power of evil. They aroused the fury of it – and so will you arouse the fury. So don't be surprised if it gets worse. Your very immovability, your very resistance, your fearlessness, arouses a passion of fury against you as a servant of Christ. So what?

'Oh,' the king said, 'we'll make it seven times hotter.'
And into the midst of that fire came the Son of God.

The Coming of the Son of God

Even Nebuchadnezzar, that heathen king who didn't
know about Christ, knew it was the Son of God. He said,
'It's like a son of the gods'; he didn't know any other way
to put it. It was the Son of God! He came into that fire!
Where was that opposition then? Where was that immovable darkness and strength then? Where were these three
bound men that were to die a terrible death in this blazing
fire? They weren't where those who had flung them in
were, dead by the heat. They were walking up and down
in the fire: the hottest place, the place that naturally would
be so much dreaded – as if 'the thing I greatly feared came
upon me'. But they hadn't feared it. They had said, 'So
what? God will be there. Whether we live or die, He'll be
there.' And He was. They would never have known it if
they had not trusted Him and experienced it. He was
better than they could have asked – but they hadn't made
any demands. And that is the hallmark, I think,
of true spirituality, of true commitment: to make no
condition whatsoever.

Into that fire came Christ. And of course when He was
there they were not bound. Nebuchadnezzar couldn't do a
thing about it. He couldn't even come near the fire; he had
to stand a great way off to look. He is terrified; he is
amazed. He says, 'We put in three men bound; there are
four walking about now, and the fourth is like the Son
of God.' He is terrified – praise God! – but in a good way.
God had mercy on him. He loved Nebuchadnezzar too; he
was only a tool. Where was that power behind him?
Destroyed by that fire.

Christ's Victory in Recent Days

I had occasion during this week to be with another. We

were very burdened about a particular situation, and we had felt to set aside some days of fasting and praying, to give concentrated attention to this. It was just like an immovable darkness. We had agreed on a time to come together to pray. When we met, we discovered that during the days of preparation we had both felt a tremendous sense of light, and we knew we were to concentrate on that light and not on the darkness. I now felt to open my being as never before, and was enabled to do it more fully than ever, to be a channel for the light of Christ. And that light began to flow. It began to flow into the darkness and pushed it further and further back until the light was blazing. As we looked, we both knew that the impenetrable, immovable spirit behind it all, behind the darkness, was still there and **hadn't moved an inch** – and was **exultant**: you could see its eyes – it was exultant; it was flaunting. It had no intention of budging a single inch. Who were we? Just two weak females praying.

And we prayed again.

Do you know, it happened so fast I can hardly tell you what happened. **It was gone, for Christ was there!** And the angelic presences were there, and they carried it out of sight. It happened so fast I couldn't even see it going until I was aware it was being carried away. It was now nothing. Believe me, it had been real; it was not our imagination. It was real, it was hellish. And it was nothing when Christ came. And oh, the presence of Christ ... I feel I have been marked with it. It has changed something, it is changing me. The presence of Christ I felt, that kingly, kingly One. I loved Him, just loved Him. I was jealous for His glory, jealous that that area would be brought to His feet. I felt that darkness and saw it go. Please God, this shall happen with more and more of us, that we will take this responsibility and will not just sense but **know** that dark powers are being broken in spiritual places. It is nothing to Christ, just nothing. Praise His Name!

And oh, the sense of the open heaven, the sense of that kingly One hovering over that whole part, the sense of

Him claiming it. And oh, His love for the place, and His intention to bless! I felt how rightfully it is His; it can be His, if we love Him enough to believe Him and not be afraid. He walked into that fire, and He walks with us. And I don't think Nebuchadnezzar saw it happen; I don't think anybody saw the moment happen when they were loosed; it just was, because Christ was there, our Christ, our Lord. He is the King. He is so bright, He is so glorious, He is so totally unopposable.

Never think that when Christ comes, there is then a fight between Him and darkness. There is not: there is no fight. It's all over! The darkness doesn't wait – it doesn't stand upon the order of its going! I have seen this again and again. You know, every time I speak like this I suffer for it afterwards. I don't care. I want you to hear it and believe it and know it! It is true. I have seen again and again, maybe in praying with a person, that the darkness appears immovable, and it seems the person is never going to get free – a person that really wants to go on, wants to be free. Suddenly Christ is there. And the evil power doesn't wait to be dismissed. It is frightened of Christ – goes before He gets too near it. Christ is so precious. There really is not anything to be afraid of. I don't say that lightly. I know what can sometimes happen. Look how far God let these three go: into a blazing furnace seven times heated. He let that happen, and He doesn't promise that He will never let something like that happen to us (maybe not physically, but spiritually). But the same will happen for us – I know it will – as did for them. Christ, Christ. I'd rather be there with Him than in a nice, easy, cosy place, with Him not very near me. I'd rather even be in there and not feel His presence, but know that He had put me there, than be, yes, even in the loveliness of His presence, but knowing that I had gone there by way of a side road and that He was taking mercy on me and being kind to me, because He is kind. I would rather be in the difficult place without the sense of His presence, if that is where He first ordained.

No Smell of Burning

And there is one further point. *They saw that the fire had not harmed their bodies, nor was a hair of their head singed; their robes were not scorched, and there was no smell of fire on them.* There was no mark on them, not even a smell of singeing on their garments. They came through an experience of stark spiritual conflict **unscathed**, unharmed. And sometimes as the fire closes round us – or, to change the metaphor, as the waves rise very high – we think we will never be the same again. It seems sometimes we have reached a depth of pain, a depth of suffering, a depth of wounding in our spirit that will never heal, that will never be totally healed. We sometimes feel we have been so marked by the hellishness of the hatred of hell that we will never be the same. And it is not true. Not a hair of them was harmed; not even their clothes, never mind their bodies, smelled of the burning. I think they were rich in the fragrance of the One who had walked with them. What an experience! I think the worst moment for them was coming out of that fire. They would have walked in it all their lives; they would have walked home with Him. A foreknowledge of the One who was going to come for us! They walked there with Christ. They loved Him.

That verse that tells us not a hair of them was singed, their robes were not scorched, and there was no smell of fire on them, reminds me of that other verse that speaks of Christ:

> *A bone of him shall not be broken.*
> (John 19:36; cf. Psalm 34:20)

And the depths of His suffering: oh, the depths of His conflict! The unutterable, unfathomable depths of the hatred of hell poured out in a concentrated fury on Christ! We know that if we are for a moment the object of Satan's annoyance or anger or hatred, he has lots of others he is bothering about far more at the same time. But it was all concentrated on this One, Jesus. And He was going to go so far down that the billows of God would close over His head. They never close over ours. He always comes down with us; He is always waiting for us at the bottom. Be honest: you have never gone right down. No matter how far you have ever gone down, hasn't He been there waiting? You didn't see Him until you were there, but He was there. And He always, always shall be. Christ went right down into the bottom of the chasm and He was broken in pieces, in the sense that He was rent: His heart was broken, as He went down, down, and the waters closed over Him. But still the prophecy held:

> *Thou wilt not suffer thy holy one to see corruption.*
> (Psalm 16:10; slightly amended)

> *Not a bone of him shall be broken.*

It speaks even more powerfully of His inner being: that pure, pure spirit, so crystal clear, so powerful because of its clearness, so rich in giving and in love, undamaged, unscathed. He bears the marks on His brow of His suffering for us, but they are beautiful marks. There is no taint on Him. There is no sense of shadow with Christ, is there? He has not come out of the depths of the conflict a shadowed One, to spread sorrow and shadow. He has come out – we cannot describe how He has come out. Oh, that we could. The Spirit shall do it for us. Shall we worship Him, as we turn to communion with our Beloved.

Appendix

Normal Fear versus Phobia

The question is sometimes asked: How do we distinguish between a healthy fear and a phobia?

The difference between a fear and a phobia is very simple. If a mighty big poisonous snake came wriggling in here now, I would have a reasonable fear and get out of its way. Now that is a good, sensible, healthy kind of fear that God has put in intelligent creatures. But it is quite different from the feeling of horror that can rise in some people at the very idea of snakes. You might be in the position that you are never likely to see a snake or be in the slightest danger from a snake, but the idea can still give you nightmares. That is a phobia. It is quite different.

Take the fear of heights. If you were employed as a slater, you would have to work at times on steep and slippery roofs. If you were an ordinary, intelligent person, you would have a healthy respect for the danger of the job. That would be a reasonable fear. But the horror of heights that many suffer from has nothing to do with the real world at all: that is a phobia.

I often say in ministering to people: 'Look. You are not really afraid of this, that or the other. What you are really experiencing is what I call the fear of the fear. Now God is not going to take away the healthy fear, which is for your good. He takes away the horror, which was not placed there by Him in the first place; it came from hell.' There can be horror associated with what starts out as a real and sensible fear. The matter is quite simple, and people who experience deliverance from a phobia distinguish very clearly between the two conditions.

Note to Readers

If you would like to enquire further about issues raised in this book or if you feel that the compiler could be of help, you are invited to write to him at 27 Denholm Street, Greenock, PA16 8RH, Scotland, or telephone 01475-729668 or 01475-787432.

It may also be of interest to know that Hugh Black is normally involved in five conferences in Scotland each year – New Year, Easter, July, August and October. Friends gather from many parts of Britain. An open invitation is extended to all and particularly to those interested in the baptism in the Holy Spirit and related themes. Details will be provided on enquiry.

Other Books by Hugh Black

The Baptism in the Spirit and Its Effects   **£4.99**

Used in bringing people into the baptism in the Spirit
and described as one of the clearest, most incisive
books on the subject. This expanded edition includes
evidence that Finney, Moody and Spurgeon spoke in
tongues, and narrates miraculous effects of the
baptism in the lives of Jimmy Lunan and Allan
Wiggins.

Reflections on the Gifts of the Spirit   **£2.75**

Deals in an original way with its subject. The chapters
on miracles, healings and discernment (with exorcism)
have roused great interest and led to positive action.
Anecdotes and illustrations have been much appre-
ciated.

Reflections on a Song of Love   **£1.25**

A highly original commentary on 1 Corinthians 13.
The drawing power of love pervades this fascinating
study. The author shows very clearly how this chapter
fully supports and in no way detracts from the doctrine
of Pentecost.

A Trumpet Call to Women £2.50

Presents a strong case from Scripture for greater involvement of women in ministry. It throws much light on those portions which on the surface seem to put women in a subject role. It includes the testimony of Elizabeth H. Taylor, a lady much used of God. A stirring book, demanding a response – a call to action.

Consider Him £2.25

Considers a number of the qualities of Christ. He Himself seems to speak from the pages of the book, both in the main text and in the testimony of Jennifer Jack, whose selfless presentation truly leaves the reader to consider Christ.

Battle for the Body £2.95

It will take courage to face the truths highlighted in this original approach to fundamental issues of sanctification. The second part presents the powerful testimony of John Hamilton – a preacher widely known and loved.

The Clash of Tongues: With Glimpses of Revival £2.75

Part One is a commentary on 1 Corinthians 14. It deals in detail with some of the more difficult questions. Part Two deals with the relationship between revival and Pentecost and refers to the 1939 and 1949 revivals in Lewis, introducing a number of people who were involved in the first of these – particularly Mary MacLean, whose remarkable testimony is related. This book may particularly appeal to people studiously inclined.

The Incomparable Christ £2.75

Part One deals with the gospel. It faces honestly the questions of Christ's resurrection and that of all men.

It deals in a direct way with the doctrine of hell and eternal judgment, and gives practical instruction on the way of salvation. Part Two presents the remarkable testimonies of two young ladies.

Gospel Vignettes £2.95

Focuses attention on various facets of the gospel, with chapter titles like: Ye Must Be Born Again, The Life-Giving Water, Weighed in the Balances, Behold I Stand at the Door and Knock, The Hour of Decision. Includes testimonies of three people whose lives have been transformed by Christ, to one of whom Christ Himself appeared. Useful in the gospel, but introducing the Pentecostal dimension.

Reflections from Abraham £2.50

Outlines spiritual principles seen in the life of Abraham. It deals with his call and ours, the mountain as distinct from the valley life, intercession, Lot in Sodom, the sacrifice of Isaac and the way of faith. Part Two tells of the action of God in the life of Dorothy Jennings, to whom Abraham has been of particular significance.

Reflections from Moses:
With the Testimony of Dan McVicar £2.99

Part One shows the outworking of spiritual principles such as the calling and training of a man of God, the need to start from holy ground, deliverance from bondage, and the consequences of Moses' failure in a critical hour. Part Two presents the well-known evangelist Dan McVicar's story in his own words. The conversion of this militant communist and the intervention of God in the lives of his parents make thrilling reading.

Christ the Deliverer   £2.99

Deals with both physical and spiritual deliverance. It includes a number of remarkable testimonies to healing, e.g. from blindness, manic depression, ME, rheumatoid arthritis, spinal injury, phobias, nightmares. It speaks of the appearance of angels, touches on revival and analyses the theory of 'visualization'.

Christian Fundamentals   £3.50

Part One deals with the individual and his needs in the realms of Salvation, Baptism in the Spirit, and Deliverance. Part Two focuses on the outflow of the life of God to meet the needs of others through Vocal, Hidden and Open Power Ministries. The End Times are the subject of Part Three.

Reflections from David   £3.75

This searching book shows a man after God's own heart in the glory of his achievements and the tragedy of his failings. Divine retribution and forgiveness, the joy of deliverance, and the action of God in present-day lives are all examined.

Pioneers of the Spiritual Way   £4.99

From a lost Eden our race walked a lost road, occasionally experiencing higher things as pioneers of the spiritual way led upwards. The impassable barrier between God and man was finally removed as the last Adam blasted a way through: Christ, bringing many sons to glory.

Revival:
Including the Prophetic Vision of Jean Darnall   £3.99

Some of the great revivals of the past are reviewed with their enduring principles and changing patterns. Revival comes nearer as we are confronted with more recent movements of God. The celebrated vision of

Jean Darnall has left many with a feeling of keen expectation for coming days.

Revival: Personal Encounters £4.50

From the treasure chest of memory the author brings a series of revival-related incidents. We hear of Studd, Burton and Salter and of revival in the Congo and Rwanda. More is revealed of the moving of God in Lewis and at an unusual Scottish school camp. A contemporary scene in Brazil brings revival very close. The highly original testimony of Alison Speirs brings the fact and challenge right to our doorstep.

Revival: Living in the Realities £3.99

For a revived or a revival-conscious people a high level of Christian living is immediately presented. The experience of revival has to be outworked. This book ponders issues such as spiritual warfare, what it means to be imitators of Christ, the need to progress from forgiveness to love for those who do us harm, and the mystery of the love of God itself. An unusual and thought-provoking approach.

E.H. Taylor: A Modern Christian Mystic:
Sayings and Recollections £4.50

A sequel to *Trumpet Call to Women*, this highly unusual book contains insights into a wide range of spiritual themes on the part of one who was much used in predictive prophecy and in leading people into the baptism in the Spirit and deliverance, and especially into a deep knowledge of Christ.

Book Orders

New Dawn Bookshop, 10A Jamaica Street, Greenock
Renfrewshire, PA15 1YB, Scotland
Telephone 01475 729668   Fax 01475 728145

ORDER FORM

Please send me books by Hugh B. Black indicated below:

Quantity	Title	Price
_____	The Baptism in the Spirit and Its Effects	£4.99
_____	Reflections on the Gifts of the Spirit	£2.75
_____	Reflections on a Song of Love (A commentary on 1 Corinthians 13)	£1.25
_____	A Trumpet Call to Women	£2.50
_____	Consider Him (Twelve Qualities of Christ)	£2.25
_____	Battle for the Body	£2.95
_____	The Clash of Tongues: With Glimpses of Revival	£2.75
_____	The Incomparable Christ	£2.75
_____	Gospel Vignettes	£2.95
_____	Reflections from Abraham	£2.50
_____	Reflections from Moses: With the Testimony of Dan McVicar	£2.99
_____	Christ the Deliverer	£2.99
_____	Christian Fundamentals	£3.50

(cont. overleaf)

_____	Reflections from David	£3.75
_____	Pioneers of the Spiritual Way	£4.99
_____	Revival: Including the Prophetic Vision of Jean Darnall	£3.99
_____	Revival: Personal Encounters	£4.50
_____	Revival: Living in the Realities	£3.99
_____	E.H. Taylor: A Modern Christian Mystic	£4.50
_____	War in Heaven and Earth	£6.99

Name . . . .

Address . . . .

. . . .

. . . . Post Code . . . .

Please add 50p per book for postage and packing.